ADAM HAMILTON'S

24 Hours
That Changed
the World

For Older Children

Jesus' Last Week on Earth

MARCIA STONER

Abingdon Press
Nashville

24 Hours
That Changed the World
For Older Children
Jesus' Last Week on Earth

Art Credits: pp. 4, 46: Rick Drennan/Storybook Arts, © 2008 Cokesbury. p. 5: Brenda Gilliam, © 2001 Cokesbury. pp. 12, 13: Paige Easter, © 2010 Cokesbury. p. 22: Art Explosion (bandage, bicycle, shovel, microphone, rake, crutches), Image Club (hammer, dog, eggs, guitar, books, money, boxes, medicine), Thinkstock (CD player). p. 28: Megan Jeffery, © 2004 Cokesbury. p. 29: Brenda Gilliam, © 2006 Cokesbury. p. 54: Rick Drennan/Storybook Arts, © 2008 Cokesbury (tree, robe, rooster); Dynamic Graphics (crown of thorns); Paige Easter, © 2010 Cokesbury (palm branch, basin and towel, chalice and bread); Randy Wollenmann, © 2004 Cokesbury (cross). p. 55: Charles Jakubowski, © 1998 Abingdon Press. pp. 63, 64: Randy Wollenmann, © 2002 Cokesbury.

Photo Credits: pp. 8, 41, 48, 59: Ron Benedict, © 2010 Abingdon Press.

Marcia Stoner lives in Nashville, Tennessee, where she is a writer and editor of children's curriculum resources. Marcia is a member of Christ United Methodist Church. She has served in local congregations as Director of Christian Education. Marcia also taught English in Hiroshima Jogakuin Jr. and Sr. High Schools in Hiroshima, Japan, for four years. She presently serves as editor of *Rock Solid: Tweens in Transition* and other tween resources at The United Methodist Publishing House.

ISBN 978-1-426-71431-3

PACP00777824-01

11 12 13 14 15 16 17 18 19—10 9 8 7 6 5 4 3 2

Printed in the U. S. A.

CONTENTS

Your church can do a church-wide study of *24 Hours* by using the younger children's resource, *24 Hours That Changed the World: Jesus' Last Week on Earth (For Younger Children)* by Daphna Flegal; the youth resource, *24 Hours That Changed the World (For Youth)* by Jason Gant; and the adult resource, *24 Hours That Changed the World* by Adam Hamilton.

Worship Prayers

Palm Sunday Prayer

Our God, we come to you today with joy in our hearts. We are thankful for your gift of Jesus, our Savior. Help us keep this joy in our hearts all week. In Jesus' name we pray. Amen.

Hand-Washing Prayer

O God, the one who created and loves us, we come with humble hearts. We thank you for those who served us today by washing our hands. Help us look every day for chances to serve others in your name. Help us keep you first in our hearts, and help us show your love to others through our service. In Jesus' name we pray. Amen.

Last Supper Prayer

God, we are happy when we can come to your table and remember Jesus. We know your Spirit is among us when we eat and drink in remembrance of your Son, Jesus. We are open for the Spirit to work in our lives. Be with us now and for evermore. In Jesus' name we pray. Amen.

Prayer for Forgiveness

God, we come to you knowing that we are like Peter. We deny you in many of our actions every day. We come asking your forgiveness, knowing that you are a forgiving God. In Jesus' name we pray. Amen.

Words of Dismissal

Go now in silence and remember Jesus, our Lord. Amen.

Easter Prayer

O God, our Lord, giver of all things, we come to you today with happy hearts. We know that your love for us is endless. Be with us now as we go out into the world. In Jesus' name we pray. Amen.

Cloak Pattern (see page 7)

Make a Palm Frond Cross

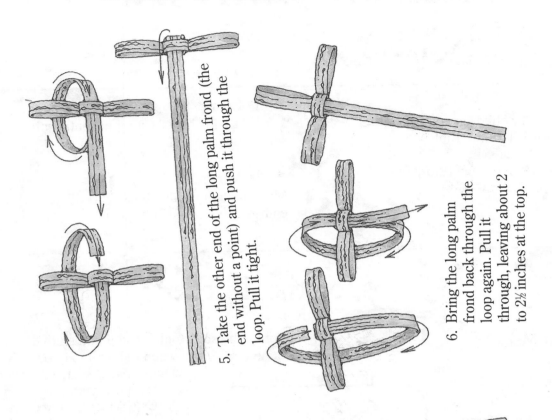

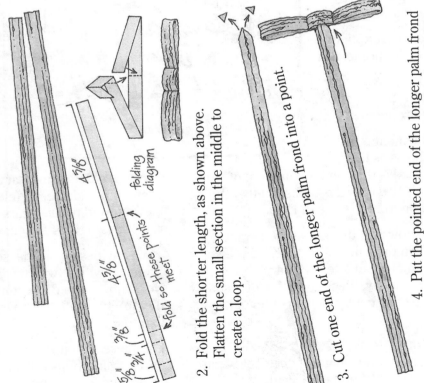

You will need:

- one short palm frond (about 11 inches long)
- one long palm frond (about 14 inches long)

1. Select two palm fronds from a palm branch.

2. Fold the shorter length, as shown above. Flatten the small section in the middle to create a loop.

3. Cut one end of the longer palm frond into a point.

4. Put the pointed end of the longer palm frond into the loop on the shorter palm frond. (Do not pull it through the loop.)

5. Take the other end of the long palm frond (the end without a point) and push it through the loop. Pull it tight.

6. Bring the long palm frond back through the loop again. Pull it through, leaving about 2 to 2½ inches at the top.

THE TRIUMPHAL ENTRY

Objectives
Older-elementary children and tweens will
• read and work with the Bible
• create Holy Week symbols
• begin a three-dimensional Holy Week Road
• recognize Jesus as the Messiah

Bible Story
Mark 11:1-11: Jesus' triumphal entry into Jerusalem

Bible Verse
Mark 11:9: Hosanna! Blessed is the one who comes in the name of the Lord!

Focus for the Teacher

What Does It Mean?

Mark is very clear in his account of Jesus' triumphal entry into Jerusalem. This is the story of the Messiah, the one sent by God to save the world.

Jesus gives exact descriptions of what the disciples are to do.

The Messiah riding on a colt (young donkey) was part of Old Testament prophecy.

The crowd itself shouts recognition of Jesus as the Messiah. ("Blessed is the coming kingdom of our ancestor David!") It was well established that the Messiah would be from the line of David.

Like Jesus, we know that this is just the beginning of a painful, difficult journey for Christ. Who Jesus is and his meaning for our lives is central to all of these lessons. For today, the recognition of Jesus as the Messiah, the one sent by God, is essential.

It's Not Palm Sunday Yet

A Lenten study, by it's very nature, does not begin on Palm Sunday, but, rather, begins with Ash Wednesday. So why start with Palm Sunday? Why

> *Hosanna! Blessed is the one who comes in the name of the Lord!*
> *Mark 11:9*

not do the study out of order and study Palm Sunday closer to when Palm Sunday actually happens? Because the events, from the triumphal entry to the Crucifixion and Resurrection of Jesus, touch the heart more deeply when experienced in the order in which they happened. Older-elementary children and tweens can understand this.

Understanding and Activities

We have carefully crafted the small-group time to the difference in maturity levels between older-elementary children (nine and ten years old) and tweens (eleven—or soon to turn eleven—and twelve years old). It is important as a rite of passage for tweens to lead worship.

The activities in each lesson build from interest group activities (which will produce the visuals for worship), to the Bible story (which is central to the theme), to small-group work, to coming back together for worship.

For interest groups, encourage participants to divide up, as craft groups will be producing things that will be needed for worship or other opportunities.

Explore Interest Groups

Be sure that adult teachers are waiting when the first child arrives. Greet and welcome each child. Get the child involved in an activity that interests him or her, and begin preparation for the day's activities. Encourage older-elementary children to make Palm Sunday symbols and tweens to help make the Jerusalem gate. Some of either age will be needed to create the sand road.

Make Palm Sunday Symbols (Older Elementary)

- **Say:** The Bible story for today is about Palm Sunday, the celebration of Jesus' triumphal entry into Jerusalem. This is the day the crowd recognized Jesus as the Messiah. We are going to work on some symbols of Palm Sunday to use in our three-dimensional Holy Week Road. Choose which of the symbols you will make.

For palm branch:

- Use the pattern to cut out the front and back of the palm branch from green felt or fabric. (It works best if cut in the same direction.)

- Use a brown marker to color a toothpick for the spine of the palm branch.

- Use fabric glue to glue the edges of the palm branch together. Leave a small opening.

- Gently pull one or two cotton balls apart, stuff them into the palm branch, and glue the opening shut.

- Glue the spine (toothpick) down the center of one side of the palm branch and press it down firmly. Set it aside to dry.

For cloak:

- Use the cloak pattern to cut out two layers of cloth. Choose one layer for the front, and cut it down the center. You may trim away part of the center to leave a small gap in the front of the cloak.

- Use fabric glue to glue the edges of the cloak all around the arms and sides of the cloak. (Do not glue the neck or hand openings, and leave the front open.) Set it aside to dry.

- Save the symbols to be placed during worship.

Prepare

✓ Photocopy the cloak and palm branch patterns (pages 4 and 12) for each child.

✓ Provide scissors, green felt or fabric, brown permanent markers, toothpicks, fabric glue, cotton balls, small pieces of scrap fabric.

Make the Jerusalem Gate (Tweens)

- **Say:** The Bible story for today is about Palm Sunday, the celebration of Jesus' triumphal entry into Jerusalem. This is the day the crowd recognized Jesus as the Messiah. We are going to work on the gate to Jerusalem through which Jesus entered. This will be used in our three-dimensional Holy Week Road.

- Invite two or three tweens to work on each half of the gate.

- Cut brown paper to a size that can be wrapped around the paper towel tube, use markers to draw lines on the paper to look like stones, wrap the tube with the paper, and secure the paper with tape.

Prepare

✓ Provide two paper towel tubes, brown paper, scissors (or paper cutter, to be used only under adult supervision), clear tape, markers, heavy paper or file folder, craft sticks, glue.

✓ Optional: For stability, cut the tubes to about eight inches.

- Cut a slit the length of a craft stick in each paper towel tube.

- Cut two pieces of heavy paper or a file folder about one half inch shorter than the length of a craft stick.

- Turn the paper so that the long sides are at the top and bottom. Fold one side over one inch. (This flap will slide into the slit on the tube.)

- Starting at the non-flap end of the paper, place a craft stick so that each end overhangs the paper. Glue it into place, and then glue other craft sticks beside it. (Do not glue any to the flap.) Glue two craft sticks across the others, about one inch from the top and bottom.

- Slide the flap of paper into the slit on the tube, and glue it to the inside. (Before gluing it into place, the two teams should make sure their half of the gate will match up with the other half. The gate will open and close.)

- Set the gate aside for closing worship.

Create a Sand Road (All)

- **Say:** The Bible story for today is about Palm Sunday, the celebration of Jesus' triumphal entry into Jerusalem. This is the day the crowd recognized Jesus as the Messiah. We are going to work on a sand road to use in our three-dimensional Holy Week Road.

- Cover the table with newspaper to protect it. Then cover the newspaper with white paper. (The kind that comes on a long roll is best, but not necessary.) Tape the paper to the table.

- Ask one child to draw two lines that are far apart to create the outline for a road. (A winding road is best.)

- Mix tempera paint with sand and a small amount of glue to color in the road, or just cover the road with glue and then cover with sand. (Remember, this has to dry before closing worship.) The road may be covered in sections, finishing in the next lesson.

- **Say:** This is the road to Jerusalem, along which Jesus traveled from his entry to his resurrection. Each week, we will travel a little along this road.

- Set the road aside to dry. It will be used during closing worship.

NOTE: You could use several pieces of white posterboard instead of paper.

Make Palm Frond Crosses (All)

- Have the children follow the directions on page 5 to make palm frond crosses.

- If you are doing *24 Hours That Changed the World (For Younger Children)*, you may want to work with their teachers to make palm frond crosses to hand out to the congregation during Palm Sunday worship. Check with other teachers about quantities being done.

- You may need to continue making crosses each lesson until there are enough for the entire congregation.

Prepare

- ✓ Set up a long table along one wall in the worship area.

- ✓ Provide old newspapers, long roll of white paper or several pieces of white posterboard, masking tape, pencil, tempera paint, sand, glue.

NOTE: If you have the powder form of the tempera paint, you will need to follow the directions to mix it with water.

Prepare

- ✓ Check with younger age level teachers and church leaders about providing crosses for the congregation.

- ✓ Make a sample palm frond cross.

- ✓ Photocopy "Make a Palm Frond Cross" (page 5) for each child.

- ✓ Provide "Make a Palm Frond Cross" reproducible, palm fronds, and scissors.

Large Group

Bring all older-elementary children and tweens together to experience the Bible story. Ring a bell or play music to alert everyone to the large-group time. Use the transition activity to move the children from the interest groups to the large-group area.

Palm Branch Tag

This game is an active, impartial way of "assigning" parts for the Bible reading activity that follows.

- Before the lesson, photocopy and cut apart the "Palm Branch Tag Cards" and attach a piece of tape to each.

- Choose one child to be IT.

- Play one round of regular tag. Then bring everyone back together and explain the new rules.

- Give IT one of the assignment cards. IT is to chase the others and, when a person is tagged, tape the assignment to that person.

- The tagged person becomes IT and is given the next assignment. Once a person has been tagged and has had a chance to be IT, that person is removed from the game.

- When all assignments have been taped to someone, everyone who remains becomes the "crowd." The crowd's role is to read Mark 11:9b (beginning with "Hosanna!") through 10 as a group with as much enthusiasm as possible.

Prepare
✓ Photocopy and cut apart the "Palm Branch Tag Cards" (page 13), and attach a piece of clear adhesive tape to each.

✓ Clear a large space for playing the game.

Dramatic Bible Reading

- Give out Bibles, and have everyone turn to Mark 11:1-11. Ask them to read their assigned parts. (Assignments are on the palm branches with which they were tagged. The crowd assignment is given above.)

- Explain that everyone is to read their assigned part from the Bible.

- Ask everyone to find their part. Remind them that they are to follow along so they will be ready to read their part at the correct time. They are to read as if this were a drama they were presenting to an audience.

- Do a practice read through.

- Remind everyone to read as dramatically as possible. If the crowd needs to rehearse reading together, have them do so.

- Ask them to read the entire Bible selection again.

- **Pray:** We, too, praise the one who comes in your name. Help us praise you in all we do. Amen.

- Quietly dismiss the children to their small groups.

Prepare
✓ Provide Bibles and reading assignments (from above activity).

Small Groups

Divide the children into small groups. The best division is between older elementary and tweens (or sophistication level). Keep the groups small, with a maximum of ten children in each group. You may need to have more than one of each group.

Older-Elementary Children

- Give each child a photocopy of "'Names for Jesus' Crossword," a Bible, and a pencil.

- **Say:** The story of Jesus' triumphal entry into Jerusalem on a donkey tells us that the people think they know who Jesus is. We're going to look at some of the names people in the Bible use for Jesus.

- Encourage the older-elementary children to work in pairs to figure out the names for Jesus using the clues and their Bibles. (The words we have used are from the NRSV Bible.)

- Then ask them to complete the crossword using the words they have discovered.

- Check the answers together. *(The answers are on page 64.)*

- **Say:** Jesus was all of the things people said he was, but the crowd on Palm Sunday made one mistake. They thought that a Messiah meant an earthly king who would come and lead them in a great revolt against an outside government (at this time, the Romans). But, instead, they got a Messiah who would sacrifice himself so that they could be part of the kingdom of God.

- Have older-elementary children prepare for their part in the large-group closing worship. While it is important for older-elementary children to participate actively in the worship, it is also an important developmental step for the tweens actually to take a lead in the worship.

- Ask those who made palm branches or cloaks to get them now.

- Explain that during worship they will place them on the road (or close to the side of the road) immediately in front of the gate, which will be placed on the table. They are to wait for a signal from you.

- If you have children who did not make palm branches or cloaks, ask them to bring chairs for everyone to sit on in front of the table. (The Holy Week Road you are creating is the worship table for all lessons.)

- When the chairs are ready, ask all to come to the worship area and sit.

Prepare

✓ Photocopy "'Names for Jesus' Crossword" (page 14) for each child.

✓ Provide Bibles, "'Names for Jesus' Crossword" reproducible, pencils.

Tweens

- Give each tween a photocopy of "Beginning and End," a Bible, and a pencil.

- **Say:** The story of Jesus' triumphal entry into Jerusalem on a donkey tells us that the people think they know who Jesus is. Do you know Jesus? One way to really know Jesus is through the practice of spiritual disciplines. One spiritual discipline is reading the Bible. We are going to use the Bible to discover some of the names for Jesus used by those who knew him or knew of him.

- Encourage the tweens to work in pairs to figure out the names for Jesus using their Bibles. They are to draw a line from the first part of the name to the second part and then to fill in the vowels of the other names for Jesus. (The words we have used are from the NRSV Bible.)

- Check the answers together. *(The answers are on page 64.)*

- **Say:** Jesus was all of the things people said he was, but the crowd on Palm Sunday made one mistake. They thought that a Messiah meant an earthly king who would come and lead them in a great revolt against an outside government (at this time, the Romans). But, instead, they got a Messiah who would sacrifice himself so that they could be part of the kingdom of God.

- Have tweens prepare for their part in the large-group closing worship.

- Decide together these assignments:
  * Placing the Jerusalem gate at the very beginning of the road and opening the gate (two volunteers)
  * Reading Mark 11:8
  * Reading Mark 11:9-10
  * Reading Mark 11a, ending with the word "temple"
  * Reading the names for Jesus (names from "Beginning and End")
  * Reading the "Palm Sunday Prayer" (Give the copy of the prayer to the volunteer now.)

- Any other tweens may help the older-elementary children place chairs for everyone to sit in, making sure there is a chair for each participant, even those who will be reading.

- Explain that at a signal from you, the gate will be brought and very gently placed at the beginning of the Holy Week Road. Once the gate is placed, each person reading the Bible will stand, in order, and read the Scripture. When done, the reader is to sit. Then the reader of the names for Jesus will stand and read the names and then sit.

- Explain that you will signal for the person reading the prayer to stand and pray at the close of worship.

- When the chairs are ready, ask all to come to the worship area and sit.

Prepare

✓ Photocopy "Beginning and End" (page 15) for each tween.

✓ Photocopy and cut apart "Worship Prayers" (page 4). Give the "Palm Sunday Prayer" to the tween volunteer.

✓ Provide Bibles, "Beginning and End" reproducible, pencils.

Large-Group Worship

Bring everyone together for a time of closing worship. Much of what you have done during this lesson leads up to worship, so it is a critical part of the lesson.

- Optional: Play music to focus everyone.

- **Say:** Today, we begin our journey through Holy Week. Our journey begins with Jesus' triumphal entry through the Jerusalem gate.

- Signal for the two volunteers with the Jerusalem gate to place it carefully at the very beginning of the road.

- Ask those assigned to read the Bible to begin.

- As the Bible verse is being read, give the signal for the older-elementary children with the palm branches and cloaks to come forward and place them on and beside the road in front of the Jerusalem gate. (Be sure to leave room for future additions to the road.)

- Signal for the reader of the names for Jesus ("Beginning and End") to read immediately after the Bible readings. (If older-elementary children are still placing their symbols, that's fine.)

- After all older-elementary children have returned to their seats, signal for the "Palm Sunday Prayer" to be read.

Prepare

✓ Optional: Set up CD player and cue the CD.

✓ Make sure all children are in place and understand the directions for their part in worship.

✓ Provide Bibles and the items made or prepared in interest group activities.

Palm Branch Pattern (see page 7)

24 Hours That Changed the World (For Older Children)

Palm Branch Tag Cards

Narrator 1:
Read Mark 11:1-2a
(ending with "and said
to them").

Jesus:
Read Mark 11:2b-3
(beginning with "Go into
the village").

Narrator 2:
Read Mark 11:4-5a
(ending with "said to them").

Bystander:
Read Mark 11:5b
(beginning with "What
are you doing").

Narrator 3:
Read Mark 11:6-9a
(ending with "were shouting").

Narrator 4:
Read Mark 11:11.

"Names for Jesus" Crossword

ACROSS
1. This word means "God is with us." (Matthew 1:23)
4. Three words (Mark 3:11)
5. Means "one who saves" (John 4:42)
6. Somebody who instructs you in something (Mark 4:38)
7. A title for God or Jesus (Mark 11:9)

DOWN
2. This word means chosen by God. The Jews were expecting him to save them. (Mark 8:29)
3. Three words meaning the Messiah was from the family of King David (Mark 10:47)

24 Hours That Changed the World (For Older Children)

Beginning and End

Match the beginnings and endings of these names for Jesus.

ALPHA AND	COUNSELOR
THE BREAD OF	DAVID
THE GOOD	GOD
LAMB OF	GOD
LIGHT OF THE	LIFE
PRINCE OF	OMEGA
SON OF	PEACE
SON OF	SHEPHERD
WONDERFUL	WORLD

What are other names for Jesus? Fill in the missing vowels to find out.
We've given you the vowels. Just mark each vowel off when you've used it.

S _ V _ _ R

M _ S S _ _ H

L _ R D

A A E I I O O

If you need help, look up the Scriptures below.

Scripture References

Isaiah 9:6	Mark 3:11	Mark 8:29	Mark 10:47
Mark 11:9	John 1:29	John 4:42	John 6:35
John 8:12	John 10:11	Revelation 1:8	Revelation 22:13

2 JESUS WASHES DISCIPLES' FEET

Objectives
Older-elementary children and tweens will
- read and work with the Bible
- create Holy Week symbols
- continue three-dimensional Holy Week Road
- begin a service project
- participate in a hand-washing worship

Bible Story
John 13:1-15: Jesus washes the disciples' feet.

Bible Verse
John 13:15: For I have set you an example, that you also should do as I have done.

Focus for the Teacher

What Does It Mean?

Like most stories in the Book of John, the story of Jesus washing the disciples' feet has many layers of meaning. We will look at the meaning of servanthood and hospitality on the lives of older-elementary children and tweens.

Foot washing was a question of hygiene in the first century. The visitor washed his own feet. Or the host would, as an act of hospitality, provide a servant to wash the visitor's feet.

> For I have set you an example, that you also should do as I have done.
> John 13:15

When Jesus took on the washing of the disciples' feet, he took on both the role of the servant and the role of hospitality, the free offering of this service. Through this action, Jesus was not only showing that serving is key to discipleship, but also that we are to welcome others to the kingdom of God.

Servanthood was central to the life, death, and resurrection of Jesus. At this time, Jesus was demonstrating that he was not only willing to serve by washing the disciples' feet, but was also willing to lay down his life that all might live.

For older-elementary children and tweens, taking on the role of servant to others because of a relationship with God is a powerful concept.

Serving Opportunities

To internalize this servanthood means to act upon it. There will be two opportunities to experience serving. One will be the service project to be undertaken over the next several lessons. The other experience will be the washing of hands during closing worship. Tweens will be given the opportunity to wash the hands of the older-elementary children. As with Jesus and Peter, it is necessary for someone to serve and for others to receive the service.

Explore Interest Groups

Be sure that adult teachers are waiting when the first child arrives. Greet and welcome each child. Get the child involved in an activity that interests him or her, and begin preparation for the day's activities. Encourage older-elementary children to make towel symbols and tweens to make the Upper Room table.

Make Towel Symbols (Older Elementary)

- **Say:** The Bible story for today is about Jesus washing the disciples' feet in the Upper Room at the Passover meal. With this action, Jesus sets an example of true discipleship. Disciples serve. We are going to make towels as the symbol of servanthood.

- Have each child do the following:
  * Cut from a piece of cloth or felt a strip that is three by six inches.
  * Fold the strip in half from side to side, fold it in half from top to bottom, and then use fingers to press in the seams.
  * Cut fringe or ribbon to fit the front edge of the towel, and use fabric glue to attach it to the "towel." (Or, if you prefer, this can be hand basted.)
  * Use fabric paints or puff paints to write the word "SERVE" on the miniature towel.

- Have them set the towels aside to dry to be used during worship.

Prepare
✓ Provide scissors; cloth or felt; fringe, ribbon, or other trim; fabric glue; ruler; fabric paints or puff paints.

Optional: Use a needle and thread to hand baste the fringe or ribbon onto the towel.

Make Upper Room Table (Tweens)

- **Say:** The Bible story for today is about Jesus washing the disciples' feet in the Upper Room at the Passover meal. With this action, Jesus sets an example of true discipleship. Disciples serve. We are going to make the table in the Upper Room.

Divide up these tasks:

- Cover two plastic CD cases with brown construction paper and then tape the paper in place.

- Measure the width of the Holy Week Road.

- Cut a piece of cardboard the width of the top edge of the CD cases and a little longer than the width of the road. Paint the top brown.

- Set the two covered CD cases on their edges, and glue the painted cardboard "tabletop" to the CD case "legs." Brace the CD legs with four narrow pieces of wood or blocks. Allow it to dry until closing worship.

Prepare
✓ Provide two used plastic CD cases, scissors, brown construction paper, clear tape, glue, measuring tape, heavy cardboard, brown paint and paintbrushes, 4 narrow pieces of wood or wooden blocks (for bracing each side of the cases).

✓ Optional: Precut three pieces of wood. Have the tweens paint the wood brown and glue them together for the table.

Continue Sand Road (All—if not finished)

- **Say:** The Bible story for today is about Jesus washing the disciples' feet in the Upper Room at the Passover meal. With this action, Jesus sets an example of true discipleship. Disciples serve. We are going to work on the section of sand road for the placement of the Upper Room table.

- Have them add the next section of road to the table in the worship area.

Prepare
✓ Provide more of the same materials used on the first section of the road.

Continue Palm Frond Crosses (All—if needed)

- If more palm frond crosses are needed, have the children follow the directions on page 5 to make them.

- Set them aside in a safe place until enough crosses are made for the congregation.

Prepare

✓ Provide "Make a Palm Frond Cross" reproducible (page 5), palm fronds, and scissors.

"Three Things" Game (All)

- **Say:** Jesus set us an example. We're going to play a game that challenges us to be creative in how we can serve others.

- Lay all the "'Three Things' Cards" face-down on the table.

- Explain that three cards will be turned over, and the first person to come up with a way to use the three together to serve someone will turn over the next three cards.

- Ask a volunteer to choose three of the cards and turn them over.

NOTE: Some things will go together more naturally than others, so some of the things they come up with will probably be funny. That's all right. The point is to get them thinking.

Prepare

✓ Photocopy and cut apart the "Three Things' Cards" (page 22).

Large Group

Bring all older-elementary children and tweens together to experience the Bible story. Ring a bell or play music to alert everyone to the large-group time. Use the transition activity to move the children from the interest groups to the large-group area.

Foot-Washing Relay

- Divide all children into two or more teams of equal numbers.

- **Say:** Jesus washed the disciples' feet at the Last Supper. We're going to race to be good servants by having a "foot-washing" relay.

- At one end of the room, place a chair and a towel for each team. Have the children line up by teams on the opposite end of the room.

- **Say:** Because of time and health issues, we won't take off our shoes and wash feet. Instead, the towel will be used to wipe off the top and sides of each person's shoes.

- Give these directions:
  * At a signal from you, the first two people in line on each team will run to the chair. One will sit in the chair, and the other will kneel and wipe off that person's shoes. Then they will reverse, with the second person sitting in the chair and the first person wiping off the shoes.

  * When both pairs of shoes have been wiped, the two players put the towel in the chair, run back to the line, and tag the next two players.

Prepare

✓ At one end of the room, place a towel (or rag) and chair for each team.

✓ Clear a large area for the game.

✓ Provide chairs and towels (or rags).

* Each pair repeats sitting in the chair and wiping off the other's shoes and then running back to the line.

* The first team to complete the relay wins.

- **Say:** Because the point of this game is serving, if at any time it is judged that a player has not properly wiped the other's shoes or does not kneel to do so, those players will have to repeat the process.

- Play the game.

Read Your Part

- Give all children a Bible, and ask them to find John 13:1-15.

- Divide children into three groups.

- Assign each group one of these three parts: Jesus, Peter, Narrator.

- Give these assignments so that they can find their parts before reading begins. Provide paper and pencils for them to record assignments.
  * Peter—John 13:6b, 8a, 9
  * Jesus—John 13:7, 8:b, 10, 11b, 12b-15
  * Narrator—The Peter and Jesus groups are to read only the quoted words. The Narrator group will read everything else, including things such as "he said."

- Give everyone time to find and mark their assignments. (Be prepared to have a teacher read with each group to make it easier for those with less-advanced reading abilities.)

- Begin the reading with the Narrator group going first.

- **Ask:** Whom did Jesus serve? *(the disciples)* What did he do? *(He washed their feet.)* Why was this unusual? *(He was their teacher.)* Why did Jesus serve them? *(Because he was setting an example of the kingdom of God, where it is important to serve one another.)*

Bless My Sole

- **Say:** Every Friday night, a few people from Centenary United Methodist Church in Richmond, Virginia, wash the feet of those in need who come to the church for a meal.

- To learn more about this ministry, go to *centumc.org/blessmysole.html*.

- If you have Internet access together, watch the YouTube video at *youtube.com/watch?v=msaU6yR3bA4*.

- Explain that a nice pair of clean socks would bring extra comfort.

- Encourage your children to bring new socks during the next few weeks to be distributed to those in need who come to your church for a meal.

NOTE: Websites are constantly changing. Although these websites were checked at the time this book was edited, we recommend that you double check the site to verify that it is still live and that it is still appropriate for children before doing the activity.

Prepare
✓ Provide Bibles, paper, and pencils.

Prepare
✓ Look up the church website and view the YouTube video. If you have the capability, set up a way to view the YouTube video as a group.

✓ Provide a large box for collecting socks.

Small Groups

Divide the children into small groups. The best division is between older elementary and tweens (or sophistication level). Keep the groups small, with a maximum of ten children in each group. You may need to have more than one of each group.

Older-Elementary Children

- Get the older-elementary children settled in their small-group area.

- **Say:** When Jesus washed the disciples' feet, he was giving us one example of serving. But we are never too young to serve others. How many ways can we think of that we can serve others?

- Encourage the older-elementary children to brainstorm ways they can serve others. Challenge them to try to think of at least ten different ways they can be servants.

- Record their responses on a dry-erase board or large sheet of paper.

- Explain that during worship, those who made towel symbols will, at a signal from you, place them on the road immediately in front of and beside the Upper Room table.

- **Say:** Today, we are going to have a small snack, and everyone is going to help. This group's task is to set up the snack area.

  Jesus set us an example of serving. In the Bible story, Jesus served; but somebody had to receive that service. Whose feet did Jesus wash? *(Peter's and the other disciples')* As the second part of our serving today, we are going to be served snacks by the other group. Our part is to be thankful and polite.

- Have them put out wet wipes or hand sanitizer bottles and make sure there are chairs. (These will need to be moved back to the worship area after the snack.) Have them wash the snack table with a clean cloth and soapy water, rinse it with clean water, and then dry it with towels.

- When the snack area has been prepared, ask them to clean their hands and find a place to sit while waiting to be served. Snacks will not be eaten until everyone is seated with a snack and a prayer is said.

Tweens

- Get the tweens settled in their small-group area.

- **Say:** When Jesus washed the disciples' feet, he was demonstrating hospitality and giving us one example of serving. As true disciples, we are to follow Jesus' example and be hospitable to others. A true disciple serves others. The washing of feet is just one example. Let's see if we can come up with fifteen different ways we can serve other people.

- Record their responses on a dry-erase board or large sheet of paper.

Prepare

✓ Work with other teachers to provide a table for large-group snacks.

✓ Provide a dry-erase board or large sheet of paper, marker, wet wipes or hand sanitizer, clean cloth, bowl with soapy water, bowl with clean water, dry towels.

Prepare

✓ Work with other teachers to provide a table for large-group snacks

✓ Give the "Hand-Washing Prayer" reproducible (page 4) to a tween volunteer.

✓ Provide a dry-erase board or large sheet of paper, marker, snack items (cookies, cheese and crackers, or whatever), juice or other drinks, small cups, plates, napkins, serving trays.

CAUTION: Be aware of food allergies the children have.

- Designate two people to place the table, which represents the Upper Room, on the Holy Week Road. Explain that during worship, you will give a signal to place the table. Give a volunteer the Bible reading assignment, John 13:12-15, and another a copy of today's prayer, "Hand-Washing Prayer."

- **Say:** Jesus set us an example of serving. In the Bible story, Jesus served; but somebody had to receive that service. Whose feet did Jesus wash? *(Peter's and the other disciples')* The older-elementary group will be setting up the snack area for us. And we are to be grateful for that service.

  Our service today will be to prepare a very simple snack and then serve it to the others. We will all eat together, but we will serve ourselves only after the other group has been served by us.

- Have the tweens clean their hands, pour drinks, and open the snacks and put them on plates to serve.

- When the snack area has been prepared, ask them to bring the snacks and drinks to the snack area and to serve the younger group first. Then they are to make sure everyone in their group has a snack. Snacks will not be eaten until everyone is seated with a snack and a prayer is said.

Large-Group Worship

Bring everyone together for a time of closing worship. Much of what you have done during this lesson leads up to worship, so it is a critical part of the lesson.

- Say a blessing, eat snacks together, and then ask the children to take their chairs to the worship area.

- Optional: Play music to focus everyone.

- **Say:** Today, we move from the gate of Jerusalem to the Upper Room. This table represents the Upper Room.

- Signal for the volunteers to place the Upper Room table a short distance down the road from the palm branches and cloaks.

- Ask the tween volunteer to read John 13:12-15.

- As the Bible is being read, give the signal for those with the towels to come forward and place them on the road immediately in front of and beside the Upper Room table.

- After all children have returned to their seats, give each adult a bucket or bowl of water and a towel.

- Ask the tweens to come forward, and have the adults wash and dry the hands of each tween. Then have the tweens wash and dry the hands of the older-elementary children.

- Close with the tween volunteer reading the "Hand-Washing Prayer."

Prepare

✓ Decide which teachers will be in charge of supervising which aspects of worship.

✓ Optional: Set up CD player and cue the CD.

✓ Provide Bibles, snacks (as outlined in small-group time), items made earlier for the Holy Week Road, buckets (or bowls) of water, towels.

"Three Things" Cards

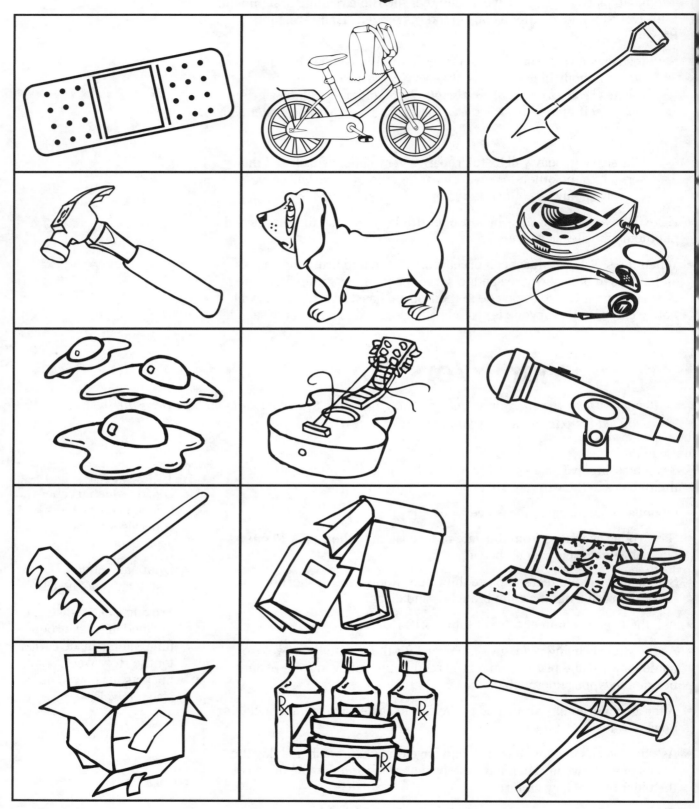

24 Hours That Changed the World (For Older Children)

3 THE LAST SUPPER

Objectives
Older-elementary children and tweens will
- read and work with the Bible
- create Holy Week symbols
- continue three-dimensional Holy Week Road
- look at the sacrament of Holy Communion
- participate in a remembrance worship

Bible Story
Luke 22:7-34: The Last Supper

Bible Verse
Luke 22:19: This is my body, which is given for you. Do this in remembrance of me.

Focus for the Teacher

Passover

The disciples were excited because they were getting ready to celebrate the Passover meal. This was a time of joy and celebration, a time when the Jewish people remembered their deliverance from slavery in Egypt and the promise that God would send a Messiah, a Savior. Jesus had been greeted with loud "Hosannas" when he entered Jerusalem on the Sunday before. The disciples were sure that Jesus was about to declare himself the Messiah.

Institution of the Lord's Supper

What happened instead astounded the disciples. During the meal Jesus took the loaf of bread, gave thanks, broke it, and gave it to the disciples. Jesus said, "This is my body, which is given for you. Do this in remembrance of me." And then he did the same with the cup. Jesus said, "This cup that is poured out for you is the new covenant in my blood." Jesus then went on to speak of the one who would betray him.

> This is my body, which is given for you.
>
> Do this in remembrance of me.
>
> Luke 22:19

The disciples began to realize that this was the beginning of the end of the earthly kingdom they had been counting on. Jesus was speaking of the end and of remembering him. Jesus talked about betrayal. Surely they couldn't be hearing correctly. And yet, they could tell that Jesus was very serious.

Jesus was telling them of what was to come, and their night of celebration turned into a time of shock, questioning, and despair.

It was in these conditions that the sacrament of Holy Communion was instituted. In this sacrament, we remember Jesus, the Son of God, the Messiah, the one who comes to show us the way to eternal life.

Older-elementary children and tweens need to begin understanding the suffering and death of Jesus so that the Resurrection has more impact. They also need to explore the sacrament of Holy Communion.

Explore Interest Groups

Be sure that adult teachers are waiting when the first child arrives. Greet and welcome each child. Get the child involved in an activity that interests him or her and introduces the theme for the day's activities. Encourage older-elementary children to make Remember Cups and tweens to make Communion Chalices.

Remember Cup (Older Elementary)

- **Say:** Today, we are going to be talking about the Last Supper, which is when Jesus began the sacrament of Holy Communion. Communion is a time when we remember Jesus. We are going to make a Remember Cup as a symbol of remembering Jesus.

- Give each child a two-inch ball of self-drying clay, and tell each child to do the following:

  * Mold the clay into any type of cup or drinking vessel the child chooses.

  * Use a toothpick to write the word "REMEMBER" in the clay cup. (The word should be deep enough so that it will be easily visible when the cup dries.)

- Set the cups aside to dry to be used in worship.

Prepare
- ✓ Provide self-drying clay and toothpicks.

Communion Chalice (Tweens)

- **Say:** Today, we are going to be talking about the Last Supper, which is when Jesus began the sacrament of Holy Communion. Communion is a time when we remember Jesus. We are going to make a Communion Chalice as part of our Holy Week Road.

- Give each tween the two pieces of a precut bottle.

- Supervise using a hot glue gun to glue the top opening (where the cap had been) to the bottom of the bottle.

- Encourage the tweens to decorate the chalice with stained-glass paints, permanent markers, sequins, beads, or any decorative trim. (This may be done before the top and bottom are glued together.)

- Set the chalices aside to dry to be used in worship.

Prepare
- ✓ Remove the lids from plastic drink bottles, and then cut the bottles in two (one per tween). You do not need to use the entire bottle and may want to cut away a portion of the center section. See the sample of a chalice on the bottom of page 29.

- ✓ Provide both halves of plastic drink bottles; hot glue gun and glue; stained-glass paints, permanent markers, sequins, beads, or any decorative trim that is easily available.

"Can You Remember?" Game (All)

- Place one container with twelve objects on a table.

- **Say:** Today, we are going to be talking about the Last Supper, which is when Jesus began the sacrament of Holy Communion. Communion is a time when we remember Jesus. We are going to test how good you are at remembering things.

- Ask everyone to pay close attention.

- Take one container and slowly pull out one object at a time and place it on the table in front of you.

- Then slowly put everything back in the container in the exact order they were removed.

- Give each child an index card or scrap piece of paper and a pencil, and ask the children to write the twelve objects they saw.

- Check their lists by again placing the objects on the table. Did anybody remember all of them?

- Take up their lists and repeat the process with the second container.

- **Ask:** Did you do better on the second round? If you did, why? *(Because they were probably paying closer attention.)*

- **Say:** To remember, we must pay attention. If we are going to remember Jesus, we must pay attention to what his life and teachings mean to us.

Dramatic Bible Reading Practice (All)

- Pass out Bibles.

- Explain that some people will do the Bible reading while others silently mime the actions described.

- Assign two skilled readers the two parts of the Scripture: Luke 22:7-13 and Luke 22:14-23.

- Assign one person the role of Jesus and two others the roles of Peter and John. Everyone else will be unnamed disciples.

- Ask the readers to read through their parts while you show Jesus and the disciples what their actions will be. For example:
  * John 22:8—Jesus points, and Peter and John seem to be questioning him (looking puzzled, looking around, shrugging their shoulders).
  * John 22:14-18—Disciples and Jesus sit down around a table. Jesus seems to be speaking, and the disciples are listening. Jesus mimes handing a cup to a disciple, and the disciples mime handing the cup around, each pretending to drink from it.

- Rehearse the reading with the actions.

Prepare
✓ Find two bags or other containers that cannot be seen through. Gather twenty-four different objects (ball, pencil, calculator, and so forth). Put twelve of the objects in one container and twelve in the other.

✓ Provide index cards or scrap paper and pencils.

Prepare
✓ Provide Bibles.

Large Group

Bring all older-elementary children and tweens together to experience the Bible story. Ring a bell or play music to alert everyone to the large-group time. Use the transition activity to move the children from the interest groups to the large-group area.

"Remember the Action" Game

- If you have a lot of children, divide them into smaller groups of no more than ten children. Have each group stand in a circle.

- **Say:** Remembering correctly takes practice, so we are going to play a game that helps us practice remembering.

- Give these instructions:

  * The first person will say his or her name and do a motion or action, such as patting knees, stomping feet, raising arms above the head, and so forth.

  * The next person repeats the first person's name and action, then says his or her name and does a different action.

  * Each person will repeat the names and actions of the people who went before and add their own name and an action. (Each action must be different.)

- Begin play, helping where needed.

Prepare
✓ none

Dramatic Bible Reading

- Have everyone but the drama participants sit where they can see what will be happening.

- Explain that they will need to pay close attention, as you will be asking them some questions about what happened.

- Have those reading the Bible stand to one side of the presentation area. (They need to stand so that they will be heard better.)

- Have them read the drama as those with mime parts mime the action.

- Have the mimes and readers join everyone else.

- **Ask:** What objects were read about? *(a jar of water—verse 10; cup and bread)* Who was present at the meal? *(Jesus and his disciples)* What did Jesus say during the meal? *(The words we hear at Communion. See John 22:14-23. Exact quotes are not necessary.)* Did Jesus name the person who was to betray him? *(no)*

- Before adjourning to small groups, remind everyone about the sock collection service project that you started in the last lesson. If anyone has brought socks, collect them now. Remind the others that you are collecting socks for people who are homeless.

Prepare
✓ Provide Bibles and the box for collecting socks.

Small Groups

Divide the children into small groups. The best division is between older elementary and tweens (or sophistication level). Keep the groups small, with a maximum of ten children in each group. You may need to have more than one of each group.

Older-Elementary Children

Prepare
✓ Provide a ball.

- Have older-elementary children sit in a circle.

- **Say:** When we take Communion in worship, we are to remember Jesus, our Savior. We're going to see how many different things we can remember about Jesus.

- Give these instructions:

  * I will begin by tossing a ball to one person. That person tosses it to someone else. Keep tossing the ball until I say "Stop."

  * Whoever is holding the ball when I say "Stop" must say one thing he or she remembers about Jesus. It can be about Jesus' life, what Jesus taught, or a miracle Jesus performed.

  * When the ball holder has said something about Jesus, he or she begins the game again by tossing the ball. Each time I say "Stop," the person holding the ball must say something about Jesus that was not said before.

  * A person who can't think of anything new may ask for help from one other person.

- Play as time allows or until everyone has had at least one chance to say something about Jesus.

- Remove the ball and ask the children if there is anything else that they remember about Jesus that is really important.

- **Say:** Jesus came to save us and to bring us closer to God. If we remember what Jesus did and taught us, we can live faithfully; and that brings us closer to God.

- Ask those who made Remember Cups to get them now. Remind them to handle them very gently, as they probably will not be dry yet. Explain that during worship, at a signal from you, they are to gently place (without knocking over the Upper Room table on the road) their Remember Cups near the table on the road and near or on the towels placed in the last lesson.

- Ask the others to arrange the chairs in the worship area.

Tweens

Prepare
✓ Practice the movements to the Bible verse on page 28 so that you can teach them easily.

✓ Give the "Last Supper Prayer" reproducible (page 4) to a tween volunteer.

- Have the tweens sit in a circle.

- **Say:** The sacrament of Communion is important to who we are as Christians. Communion is remembering Jesus—the person as well as the Savior. Through Communion, we are remembering that God came to us and suffered and died for us—not just for the disciples of long ago, but for each of us here today. When we remember that Jesus died for us and we choose to follow him, we are given and accept God's grace and mercy through the Holy Spirit.

- Ask the tweens to think of one thing they remember that has happened to them that they think is important.

- Ask a few tweens to tell what they remember.

- **Say:** All of these things are important, but nothing is more important than our relationship with God. That is why remembering through Communion is so important. Jesus came to bring us closer to God. We are asked to remember and to respond.

- Explain that they will be leading worship with special movements to the Bible verse. In order to do that, they will need to practice.

- Lead them through the movements below several times until they can remember them.

- Ask those who made Communion Chalices to get them now. Remind them to handle them very gently, as they probably will not be dry yet. Explain that during worship, at a signal from you, they are to gently place (without knocking over the Upper Room table on the road) their Communion Chalices in a line on the edge of the road, near the Upper Room table and facing toward the worshipers. If your Upper Room table is made of wood and sturdy enough, ask one volunteer to place his or her chalice very gently on the Upper Room table.

- Explain that you will be reading the Bible verse as they do the movement.

- Give the "Last Supper Prayer" reproducible to one volunteer to be read.

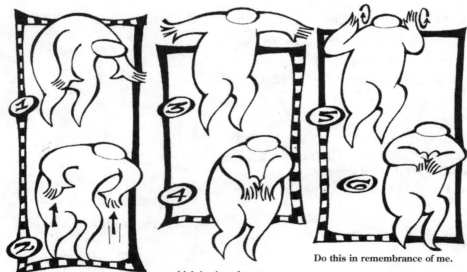

This is my body,

1. Bend gently at the waist, fingers pointed toward the floor, head down.

2. As you slowly stand, lightly trace the sides of your legs and body up to your shoulders.

which is given for you.

3. Swing arms out to the sides.

4. Then extend arms forward until your hands meet.

Do this in remembrance of me.

5. Raise extended hands together until they are almost overhead. Separate them and, with palms flat and facing either side of your head, make two circles as though your ears were the center points.

6. Then bring your hands together in front of your body and draw them into your chest.

Large-Group Worship

Bring everyone together for a time of closing worship. Much of what you have done during this lesson leads up to worship, so it is a critical part of the lesson.

- Optional: Play music to focus everyone.

- **Say:** Today, we come before this table, which represents the Upper Room. On Thursday of Holy Week, Jesus washed his disciples' feet and together they shared the Passover meal. The Passover meal was a remembrance of the Jews being freed from slavery in Egypt. In the Upper Room, Jesus instituted the sacrament of Holy Communion, a new remembrance that Jesus was about to suffer and die to save us from sin and death.

- Signal for the older-elementary children with Remember Cups to place them near the Upper Room table.

- When the older-elementary children are seated, signal for the tweens to place their Communion Chalices.

- **Say:** Today, we remember Jesus in the Upper Room with his disciples.

- Ask the tweens to come forward to prepare for the movement to the Bible verse.

- Read the Bible verse as the tweens do the movement.

- Close with the tween volunteer reading the "Last Supper Prayer."

Prepare

✓ Optional: Set up CD player and cue the CD.

✓ Provide Bibles and items made for the Holy Week Road.

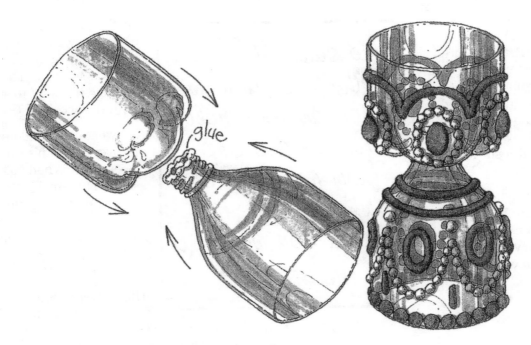

Communion Chalice (see page 24)

4 THE GARDEN OF GETHSEMANE

Objectives

Older-elementary children and tweens will
- experience the Bible story
- create Holy Week symbols
- continue three-dimensional Holy Week Road
- talk about the purpose of prayer
- participate in individual, silent prayer

Bible Story

Mark 14:26-42: Jesus prays.

Bible Verse

Mark 14:36: He said, "Abba, Father, for you all things are possible; remove this cup from me; yet, not what I want, but what you want."

Focus for the Teacher

Desertion Foretold

After Jesus and the disciples finished their Passover feast, they sang a hymn and then went to the Mount of Olives.

Before Jesus went into the garden to pray, he told his closest friends, the disciples, that they would desert him in his hour of need. The disciples were upset, and Peter declared that he would never desert him. Jesus told Peter that that very night, before the cock crowed twice, Peter would deny Jesus three times. Peter was upset and denied it. But Jesus knew the disciples well.

Even knowing this, Jesus did not condemn them. If Jesus did not condemn even his closest friends' temporary betrayal, then surely when we are momentarily weak, we will not be condemned.

> He said, "Abba, Father, for you all things are possible; remove this cup from me; yet, not what I want, but what you want."
> Mark 14:36

In the Garden

Jesus went into the garden of Gethsemane to pray. With him he took Peter, James, and John. These three were closest to Jesus and were taken with him when something special was about to occur. (All three were at the Transfiguration.)

The Scripture tells us that Jesus was deeply grieved and went to pray, struggling with what was to come. Though Jesus did not want to suffer and die, Jesus accepted God's will.

And what happened next? He discovered that his three closest friends had fallen asleep. This small betrayal in his time of greatest need was a feeling most of us, even children, have experienced. Have you ever been the one left holding the bag? Jesus was.

Things were about to get even more difficult for Jesus, but he gave himself over to God, knowing that his sacrifice would set us free from slavery to sin and death, if we too are willing to turn our lives over to God's will.

Explore Interest Groups

Be sure that adult teachers are waiting when the first child arrives. Greet and welcome each child. Get the child involved in an activity that interests him or her and introduces the theme for the day's activities. Encourage older-elementary children to make a prayer shawl and tweens to create the garden.

Make a Prayer Shawl (Older Elementary)

- **Say:** Today, we are going to hear the story of Jesus praying in the garden of Gethsemane. Using a prayer shawl is a tradition. Often, prayer shawls are knitted and given to people to celebrate the birth of a baby or to bring them comfort when they are sick or have had a death in the family. We are going to make a prayer shawl as a symbol of Jesus' prayer in the garden.

- Have the children work together to make one long "quilted" prayer shawl.

- Give them scraps of a variety of material (if available) or one large piece of material and scissors.

- Have them cut shapes. (If they prefer, they may trace a shape on the reverse side of the material to help with cutting.) They may use any shapes they want: squares, rectangles, circles, or triangles.

- Then give them needles that are already threaded, and show them how to sew the shapes together with a simple basting stitch.

- Make the shawl as long and as wide as time permits.

- Set the shawl aside to use during worship.

Prepare
✓ Provide scissors, scraps of material, and threaded needles.

Create the Garden (Tweens)

- **Say:** Today, we are going to hear the story of Jesus praying in the garden of Gethsemane. Right now, we are going to create a small symbolic garden for our Holy Week Road. We will create the garden on the road now, as it will be too fragile to move.

- Divide up these tasks among those helping to create the garden:

  * Cover a 6-by-6 inch piece of foam core with any kind of green paper. Glue the paper to the foam core. This is the base of the "garden." Place the base on the Holy Week Road now before flowers and trees are added.

  * Use small twigs, reindeer moss, and glue to make trees and bushes. Twigs may be broken to the appropriate size. Reindeer moss tears apart and is easily clumped to make trees. Glue the molded bits of reindeer moss to the twigs.

  * Cut chenille stems short. Tear small pieces of colored tissue paper, and glue them in small wads or clumps to the tops of the chenille stems to make flowers. (Optional: Purchase small "floral bouquets" from the craft store, and gently tear them apart.)

Prepare
✓ Provide a 6-by-6 foam core square, green paper, craft glue, small twigs, reindeer moss (available at craft stores), chenille stems, colored tissue paper, and toothpicks.

Optional: Purchase small "floral bouquets" from a craft store to use for the flowers. Use small gravel to make a path through the garden.

* Have those who made trees and flowers push them down into the foam core to create a garden look. A toothpick will be needed to poke the hole in the foam core before inserting the trees and flowers.

* Optional: Use small gravel to make a path through the garden.

Make a Life-size Praying Figure (All)

Prepare

✓ Provide a large piece of paper, a pencil, and markers.

* This project takes a minimum of four people.

* **Say:** Prayer is important to our relationship with God. When Jesus needed to pray, he often withdrew and went someplace quiet where he could be alone with God. We are going to make a life-size outline of a person praying to remind us we are always connected to God through prayer.

* Give these instructions:

* One volunteer will kneel with head bowed and palms together in front of his or her face in the traditional prayer position.

* Two or more people will hold the paper very close behind the person who is kneeling. The paper must be held as still as possible.

* Another person will use a pencil to draw an outline of the kneeling person on the paper. (CAUTION: Do not get too close to the person's skin. A rough outline is enough.)

* Lay the paper on the floor or on a table, and use markers to darken the pencil outline.

* Explain that you have tape ready and that, during closing worship, they will work together to hang the praying figure somewhere near the worship area.

Pass the Cup Game (All)

Prepare

✓ Write the words of Mark 14:36 on paper slips (one word per paper), fold each paper slip, put the paper slips in a cup, and mix them up.

✓ Provide a Bible and a timer or watch with a second hand.

* Read Mark 14:36.

* **Say:** When Jesus went to the garden of Gethsemane to pray, he asked God to keep him from being tested. But he knew that God's will must be obeyed. We're going to see how much of the Bible verse you remember.

* Explain that you will pass a cup containing slips of paper. Each paper has one word of today's Bible verse written on it. When they get the cup, they are to take one word.

* Continue passing the cup until all words have been drawn.

* Have the children race against time to put the Bible verse together in order.

* If you have time, do it again to see if they can beat their own time.

Large Group

Bring all older-elementary children and tweens together to experience the Bible story. Ring a bell or play music to alert everyone to the large-group time. Use the transition activity to move the children from the interest groups to the large-group area.

Prayer Tag

- Spread the "prayer" papers around the floor as far apart as possible. Tape them to the floor for stability. You will need two fewer than there are participants.

- Choose one person to be IT.

- Explain that when the music begins, everyone is to move around the room. When the music stops, everyone is to find the nearest "prayer" paper and kneel on it. Only a person who is not kneeling on a paper can be tagged. When a person is tagged, that person becomes IT.

- Begin play.

- At the end of each round, remove one to three papers (depending on time and the size of the group), adding to the number of children who can be tagged.

- **Say:** Prayer doesn't protect you from the bad things that happen in life, but it does give you the strength to go through the tough times.

Listen to the Bible Reading

- Ask everyone to be seated, and divide them into three groups.

- **Say:** I am going to read the Bible story. Pretend that you are in the garden with Jesus. I want Group 1 to think about the sounds that might be heard—not just talking, but other sounds. Group 2 is to think about what smells you might notice. And Group 3 is to think about the feel of things you might touch or might touch you while in the garden. We will talk about these after the reading.

- Ask everyone to sit with their feet on the floor, their hands in their laps, and their eyes closed.

- Have everyone inhale deeply and exhale very slowly. Repeat five times.

- Read the Bible story, Mark 14:26-42.

- Ask for volunteers from each group to report what they heard, smelled, or felt.

- **Ask:** Why do you think Jesus went to the garden to pray? *(He needed some alone time with God. He didn't need distractions.)*

- Remind everyone about the sock collection project. If anyone has brought socks, collect them now. Remind the others that you are still collecting socks for people who are homeless.

Prepare

- ✓ Gather pieces of construction paper (two fewer than participants). On each piece, write "prayer." Spread them around the floor as far apart as possible, and use masking tape to attach them to the floor.

- ✓ Provide a CD player and a CD.

Prepare

- ✓ Provide a Bible and the box for collecting socks for homeless people.

Small Groups

Divide the children into small groups. The best division is between older elementary and tweens (or sophistication level). Keep the groups small, with a maximum of ten children in each group. You may need to have more than one of each group.

Older-Elementary Children

- Have older-elementary children sit where they can write.

- Give each child a copy of "Prayer" and a pencil.

- Have them look at "Prayer Promise," which is on the top of the page.

- **Say:** Below each blank line are two numbers. The first number refers to how many rows down you are to count on the grid. The second number refers to how many rows you are to count across on the grid. The space on the grid where the two numbers meet tells you the letter that goes on that blank line.

- Help everyone with the first blank line as an example, and then give them time to decode the promise. *(Answer: "The LORD is near to all who call on him." Psalm 145:18a, NRSV)*

- **Say:** Jesus prayed in the garden alone. But God is with us no matter where and when we call on God. Now let's discover where some other Bible people prayed.

- Ask them to look at "Who Prayed Where?" on the bottom of the page.

- Explain that you will read the four Scriptures and that they are to see if they can correctly match the people to where they prayed. The Scriptures are Daniel 6:10; Jonah 2:1; Luke 2:36-37; Acts 12:11-12.

- Go over the answers together. *(Answers are on page 64.)*

- **Say:** As you see, you can talk to God at any time in any situation and God will be with you.

- Ask two volunteers who worked on the prayer shawl to get it now. Explain that during worship, at a signal from you, they will drape the shawl from one side of the worship table to the other (on one side of the "garden" from front to back on the table). Remind them to be careful not to knock over anything on the table.

Tweens

- Have tweens sit where they can write, and give each a Bible, a copy of "Why Did They Pray?" and a pencil.

- **Say:** Jesus prayed in the garden because he knew that bad things were about to happen. But people pray for all kinds of reasons. We are going to search the Bible for some reasons people prayed.

- Ask the tweens to work in groups of two or three to match the people with why they prayed.

Prepare

- ✓ Photocopy "Prayer" (page 36) for each child.

- ✓ Provide Bibles, "Prayer" reproducible, and pencils.

Prepare

- ✓ Mark areas around the room (with masking tape, a piece of paper, or a chair) where tweens can create prayer spaces.

- ✓ Photocopy "Why Did They Pray?" (page 37) for each tween.

- ✓ Provide Bibles, "Why Did They Pray?" reproducible, pencils, items for prayer spaces (things such as prayer books, hymnals, flowers, candles, and maybe some artwork—anything you have on hand that might be used to create a prayer space).

- Go over the answers together. *(Answers are on page 64.)*

- **Say:** The Bible shows us that you can talk to God at any time and in any situation, and God will be with you.

- Have areas in the room marked in some way (with masking tape, a piece of paper, or a chair) where tweens may create prayer spaces—as many different spaces as your room can handle. The spaces can be close together.

- Encourage tweens to choose from available items to create prayer spaces.

- **Say:** Prayer is important to our relationship with God. When Jesus needed to pray, he often withdrew and went someplace quiet where he could be alone with God. We're going to create some prayer spaces in this room where we can go for quiet prayer time.

  Choose a space and items you want to put in that space. You should create a space that would be helpful in focusing on God. Because there are more people than spaces, we need to provide for more than one person in a space.

- Depending on the number of tweens, they can work individually, in pairs, or in small groups.

Large-Group Worship

Bring everyone together for a time of closing worship. Much of what you have done during this lesson leads up to worship, so it is a critical part of the lesson.

- Ask those with the prayer shawl to drape it over the table now.

- Ask those who made the prayer figure to use masking tape to hang it on the wall in the area designated by you earlier.

- **Say:** Today, we are going to take time to be alone with God.

- Give everyone a copy of "Prayer Helps."

- Explain that they will be spending five minutes in silent prayer, talking with God about anything that is important to them, and that you are giving them "Prayer Helps" to use if they need them.

- Ask them to divide up among the different prayer spaces. They are to sit in the prayer spaces as far from one another as possible.

- Give them five minutes for silent prayer.

- Close with everyone seated in the prayer spaces and saying together the Lord's Prayer (on the "Prayer Helps" reproducible).

Prepare

✓ Photocopy "Prayer Helps" (page 38) for each child.

✓ Make sure the prayer spaces are ready.

✓ Provide the "Prayer Helps" reproducible, items made for worship, masking tape, and items for prayer in the prayer spaces.

Prayer

Prayer Promise

Use the grid below to decode a Bible Prayer Promise.

	1	2	3	4
1	A	B	C	D
2	E	F	G	H
3	I	J	K	L
4	M	N	O	P
5	Q	R	S	T
6	U	V	W	X
7	Y	Z	.	

54 24 21 74 34 43 52 14 74 31 53 74

42 21 11 52 74 54 43 74 11 34 34 74 63 24 43

74 13 11 34 34 74 43 42 74 24 31 41 73

Who Prayed Where?

Draw a line from the person who prayed to the place he or she prayed.

Anna	in the belly of a large fish
Daniel	in the home of Mary, the Mother of Mark
Early Christians (praying for Peter)	in an upper room with open windows
Jonah	in the Temple

Why Did They Pray?

Read the Scripture, and then fill in the blank spaces on the chart.
The answers are below, but the order is mixed up.

SCRIPTURE	WHO PRAYED	PRAYED FOR	REQUEST
Genesis 18:23-24		righteous people of Sodom	
Numbers 12:10-13		Miriam	
1 Kings 3:9-10		himself	
Luke 23:33-34		those who crucified him	
Acts 12:5		Peter	
Ephesians 3:14-19		the Ephesian church (readers of the letter)	

WHO PRAYED	REQUEST
Paul early church Jesus Moses Solomon Abraham	release from prison for recovery from leprosy save city if a righteous man could be found to strengthen their faith an understanding mind to be a better king God's forgiveness for their actions

Prayer Helps

The Lord's Prayer

Our Father, who art in heaven,
   hallowed be thy name.
   Thy kingdom come,
   thy will be done on earth as it is in heaven.
Give us this day our daily bread.
And forgive us our trespasses,
   as we forgive those who trespass against us.
And lead us not into temptation,
   but deliver us from evil.
For thine is the kingdom, and the power, and the glory,
   forever. Amen.

From "The Ritual of the Former Methodist Church," in *The United Methodist Hymnal* (1989), #895.

The Prayer of Saint Francis

Lord, make me an instrument of thy peace;
where there is hatred, let me sow love;
where there is injury, pardon;
where there is doubt, faith;
where there is despair, hope;
where there is darkness, light;
and where there is sadness, joy.

O Divine Master,
grant that I may not so much seek
to be consoled as to console;
to be understood, as to understand;
to be loved, as to love;
for it is in giving that we receive,
it is in pardoning that we are pardoned,
and it is in dying that we are born to eternal life.

By Francis of Assisi, from *The United Methodist Hymnal* (1989), #481.

Talking With God

You can talk to God about

• what is making you happy

• what is making you sad

• what you are worried about

• what you are excited about

• things you don't understand

• things you're afraid of

• help you need with a problem

• something that is exciting to you

• someone you are worried about

• anything at all

24 Hours That Changed the World (For Older Children)

5 ARREST AND PETER'S DENIAL

Objectives

Older-elementary children and tweens will
- read the Bible
- create Holy Week symbols
- continue three-dimensional Holy Week Road
- experience worship that includes repentance and words of assurance

Bible Story

Mark 14:43-72: Jesus' arrest and Peter's denial

Bible Verse

Mark 14:72c: He broke down and wept.

Focus for the Teacher

Jesus' Arrest

When Jesus had finished praying in the garden of Gethsemane, he returned to Peter, James, and John and said that the hour had come. His betrayer was there.

Judas arrived in the garden along with a crowd armed with swords and clubs. It was a religious group, as the chief priests, scribes, and elders were present. Judas betrayed Jesus with a kiss. Jesus was arrested and, as he had predicted, deserted by the disciples. But let us not be too hasty in condemning the disciples. They could not have helped Jesus; and because they survived, they were able to carry on his work.

Nevertheless, in his hour of greatest need, Jesus was alone. He was taken before the council. Some people stood up and gave false testimony against him. Jesus did not answer his accusers, but stood silent.

Peter's Denial

Peter had followed Jesus from a distance and was in the courtyard below while Jesus was before the

> He broke down and wept.
> Mark 14:72c

council. A servant girl questioned him and said she thought he was with Jesus. Twice, Peter denied it. Again, bystanders said that Peter was with the Galilean, and he denied it. Just as Jesus had predicted, Peter denied Jesus three times before the cock crowed twice.

When Peter realized what had happened, he broke down and wept, for it was the one thing he had been sure he would not do. He had denied Jesus. To Peter's credit, this was the last time he denied Jesus. Peter became the strongest of the disciples and their spiritual leader after the Resurrection. Peter never again failed Jesus.

God knows that we, too, are going to falter in faith. Sometimes, we are going to be afraid and do the wrong thing. When that happens, we will be forgiven. However, like Peter, we are expected to grow in faith and abilities. We will always struggle to do right. We will be forgiven when we ask, but our regret and our attempts to do better must be genuine. God knows our hearts.

Explore Interest Groups

Be sure that adult teachers are waiting when the first child arrives. Greet and welcome each child. Get the child involved in an activity that interests him or her and introduces the theme for the day's activities. Encourage older-elementary children to make the rock wall and tweens to help make the rooster.

Make a Rock Wall (Older Elementary)

- **Say:** Today's story is about Jesus' arrest and how Peter denied knowing Jesus three times before the rooster crowed twice. For our Holy Week Road, we are going to make a rock wall for the rooster to sit on.

- Give the children a pile of stones and some glue. (If you don't have stones available, craft stores have bags of polished stones.)

- Have the children do the following to build a wall:

  * Decide how wide the wall should be. (The wall will have to be built directly on the road. Have it face the front, just in back of the sand road. It will need a wide base that is at least three to four stones deep to support the upper wall and to hold a rooster.)

  * Put glue and place stones on the paper in back of the road to make the base of the wall. Reserve some flatter stones for the top of the wall so that the rooster will balance properly.

  * Place the remaining stones carefully, one at a time, until the wall is four or five stones high.

  * Let the wall dry in place.

- Explain that the rooster will be placed on the wall during worship.

Prepare
✓ Provide stones (picked up or bought at a craft store) and craft glue.

Create a Rooster (Tweens)

- **Say:** Today's story is about Jesus' arrest and how Peter denied knowing Jesus three times before the rooster crowed twice. The rooster is the symbol of this betrayal. For our Holy Week Road, we are going to work together to make a rooster.

- Divide up these tasks, making sure the tweens wear plastic gloves while doing them:

  * Spray both styrofoam balls with spray paint for plastic. (WARNING: Do not use regular spray paint, as it will melt the styrofoam.)

  * Break a small craft stick and push it into the round styrofoam ball (head) and then into the egg-shaped styrofoam ball (body) to connect them.

  * Break two more small craft sticks and push them up into the rooster's body to make legs.

  * Hold the rooster while another tween carefully pushes the sharp end of feathers into one end of the egg-shaped styrofoam ball to form the tail feathers and into the sides to form wings.

Prepare
✓ Purchase small glue erasers of any shape, and cut a small slit in each with a razor blade.

✓ Provide (for number of roosters you desire made) small, round styrofoam ball; slightly larger oval styrofoam ball; spray paint for plastic (not regular spray paint); small, thin craft sticks; craft glue; feathers (from a craft store); scissors; red construction paper; pin with a bead top; small glue erasers with slits precut; plastic gloves; thin cardboard.

* Cut some feathers shorter, and push them into the circle to make the rooster's comb.

* Make a beak by cutting a piece of red construction paper into a small square and then folding the paper in half one direction and then in half the other direction. Cut into a triangle from the point to the fold. (Trim if necessary.) Attach with a straight pin that has a bead top.

* Place the rooster's legs into the slits in the small erasers to make feet.

* Put a drop of glue on each place a craft stick is attached to styrofoam or the erasers. This will provide extra stability.

* If the rooster is wobbly, you may glue the feet to a small piece of thin cardboard.

• If you have large numbers of tweens, extra roosters may be made to decorate the room; but only one will be placed on the wall on the Holy Week Road.

• Explain that a volunteer will carefully place the rooster on the wall during worship.

• Have them carefully set the rooster aside to dry for worship.

Opposite Game (All)

• **Say:** Peter was weak when he denied knowing Jesus. Peter was upset with himself. But when Peter realized that Jesus had forgiven him, his weakness turned into strength. Peter became strong and continued to be strong all his life. He became the opposite of weak.

• Divide the children into two teams, and have the teams sit facing each other.

• Explain that you will toss a ball. The child who catches the ball will have to say a word—for example, "loud"—and then toss the ball to someone on the opposite team. The child who catches it will have to say the opposite word—for example, "quiet"—and then say another word and toss the ball back to the other team.

• The child on that team then has to say the opposite of the new word.

• If a player has a problem thinking of a word or its opposite, other team members may help.

Prepare
✓ Provide a ball (or balls if you have a large number of children).

Drama Practice (All)

• Pass out copies of "Peter Wept."

• Assign the roles of the Bible drama.

• Give everyone a chance to find and mark the parts.

• Have them practice reading the parts.

• If desired, give stage directions so that it can be acted out as well as read.

• Practice as time allows.

Prepare
✓ Make photocopies of "Peter Wept" (page 45) for each drama participant.

✓ Decide on staging directions.

✓ Provide "Peter Wept" reproducible and pencils.

Large Group

Bring all older-elementary children and tweens together to experience the Bible story. Ring a bell or play music to alert everyone to the large-group time. Use the transition activity to move the children from the interest groups to the large-group area.

Second-Chance Tag

- **Say:** Peter messed up when he denied that he knew Jesus, but he was given a second chance and became the leader of the Christian church. We're going to have a little fun practicing second chances.

- Pick someone to be IT, and then explain these rules:

  * IT stands between the two lines. At a signal, everyone else runs from behind one line and tries to cross over the other line without getting tagged by IT.

  * Those who get tagged go to the middle with IT and help IT tag other players.

  * At the next signal, everyone else runs back to the other line again.

  * The game will continue this way until I shout, "You are forgiven." When I shout this, everyone gets a second chance to be a runner. I will choose a new IT at that time.

- Play as long as time allows.

Prepare

✓ Using masking tape, make two parallel lines on the floor as far apart as possible. Make the lines at least ten feet long.

Bible Drama

- **Say:** Today, we are not going to read about Peter's second chance, but, rather, we are going to talk about the chance he blew. Remember, in our last lesson, we read about Jesus praying in the garden of Gethsemane. That's where we pick up today's story.

- Have those who rehearsed the drama present it to the entire group.

- **Ask:** Who betrayed Jesus? *(Judas)* Who denied he knew Jesus? *(Peter)* Why do you think Peter denied knowing Jesus? *(He was afraid.)* Why do you think Jesus gave Peter another chance later? *(Because Peter really loved Jesus, and Peter repented of his actions.)*

- **Say:** Judas didn't get a second chance, because he committed suicide quickly after he betrayed Jesus. Peter didn't get his second chance until after the resurrection of Jesus. But when Peter's opportunity for a second chance came, he took it and was a faithful follower the rest of his life.

- If anyone has brought socks, collect them now. Remind everyone that next week will be the final time for bringing in socks for people who are homeless.

- Dismiss the children to their small groups.

Prepare

✓ Set up an area where the drama can be presented and the "audience" can see and hear clearly.

✓ Provide "Peter Wept" reproducible (one per drama participant) and the box for collecting socks.

Optional: Provide costumes and props.

Small Groups

Divide the children into small groups. The best division is between older elementary and tweens (or sophistication level). Keep the groups small, with a maximum of ten children in each group. You may need to have more than one of each group.

Older-Elementary Children

- Encourage older-elementary children to sit on the floor or around a table, and give each pair of children a copy of "Rooster's Tail" (top of page 46), scissors, and glue or clear tape.

- **Say:** Peter denied Jesus when he didn't see him, but there are ways we deny Jesus, too. Often, it's by words or actions.

- Encourage the children to work in pairs to cut out the feathers of the "Rooster's Tail" and glue or tape them on the rooster.

- **Say:** These are ways we often deny Jesus as our Lord. Let's figure out what we could do instead so that we can be loyal to Jesus.

- Give several children pieces of construction paper, and have them each cut out a feather for the larger rooster by using the feathers as a sample.

- Pick one feather on the "Rooster's Tail" reproducible, and have the children decide how they could act in a way that would honor Jesus instead of denying Jesus in the way listed on the feather.

- Ask one of the children who cut out tail feathers to write what was said (a short version of two or three words) on the "feather" and glue or tape it to the larger rooster.

- Repeat until all feathers have been completed and are on the rooster.

- To keep things moving, you can move onto the second feather while the first is being glued or taped in place, and so forth.

- Explain that they will have no special duties during worship, since they have already placed the wall on the Holy Week Road.

- Have the children bring chairs to the worship area.

Tweens

- Encourage tweens to sit on the floor or around a table, and give each a copy of "I Deny Jesus" (bottom of page 46) and pencils.

- **Say:** Peter denied Jesus when he didn't see him, but there are ways we deny Jesus, too. Often, it's by words or actions.

- Explain that every time we do one of the actions shown in these examples, we deny Jesus. We are being like Peter.

- Encourage them to work in pairs to come up with ways they can honor Jesus in these types of situations.

Prepare

- ✓ Enlarge a copy of the rooster in "Rooster's Tail," and post it where it can be seen.

- ✓ Photocopy "Rooster's Tail" (page 46) for each pair of children, and cut off "I Deny Jesus" at the bottom of the page. Give the copies of "I Deny Jesus" to the person leading the tweens small group.

- ✓ Provide "Rooster's Tail" reproducible (one for every two children), scissors, glue or clear tape, construction paper, markers.

Prepare

- ✓ Photocopy "I Deny Jesus" (page 46), and cut off "Rooster's Tail" at the top of the page. Give the copies of "Rooster's Tail" to the person leading the older-elementary small group.

- ✓ Give the "Prayer for Forgiveness" reproducible (page 4) to a tween volunteer.

- ✓ Provide a Bible, "I Deny Jesus" reproducible, and pencils.

- When they have had some time to work on their answers, go over the situations one at a time and see how many different suggestions were made for each.

- Ask the tween who will be placing the rooster on the wall on the Holy Week Road to get it now.

- Ask a volunteer to look up Mark 14:72 and be ready to read the entire verse.

- Give the "Prayer for Forgiveness" reproducible to one volunteer to be read.

Large-Group Worship

Bring everyone together for a time of closing worship. Much of what you have done during this lesson leads up to worship, so it is a critical part of the lesson.

- Ask the person with the rooster to place it on the stone wall on the Holy Week Road as the Scripture verse is read.

- Ask the volunteer who will read the Scripture verse (Mark 14:72) to begin.

- When these two are seated again, ask the volunteer who will be reading the "Prayer for Forgiveness" to begin.

- **Say:** In Jesus' name you are forgiven. Amen.

Prepare
✓ Make sure the rock wall and the rooster are ready.

✓ Provide a Bible and the "Prayer for Forgiveness" reproducible.

Peter Wept

Narrator 1: It is Thursday night, and Jesus has been praying in the garden of Gethsemane. Peter, James, and John had gone with Jesus to the garden, but it was late and they fell asleep. Jesus returns to them.

Jesus: Are you still sleeping and taking your rest? Enough! The hour has come; the Son of Man is betrayed into the hands of sinners. Get up, let us be going. See, my betrayer is at hand.

James/John: What? Oh, sorry about that. We didn't mean to fall asleep.

Peter: Oh, no! So soon. They are coming for you now?

Narrator 2: Immediately, Judas arrived with a crowd with swords and clubs. In the crowd were the chief priests, scribes, and elders. Judas kissed Jesus on the cheek so they would be sure which man to arrest. One who stood near Jesus drew a sword and tried to defend him.

Jesus: Let the scriptures be fulfilled.

James: We better get out of here.

Peter: I hate to run, but we'll all be arrested if we don't get going.

John: I see a way out. Follow me!

Narrator 1: Jesus was taken to the high priest, and the council assembled.

Narrator 2: Some people stood up and testified falsely against Jesus.

High Priest: *(stands up)* Have you no answer? What is it that they testify against you? Are you the Messiah, the Son of the Blessed One?

Jesus: I am; and you will see the Son of Man seated at the right hand of the Power.

Narrator 1: This angered the high priest, and the council condemned Jesus.

Narrator 2: Meanwhile, Peter had come out of his hiding place and followed Jesus to the courtyard of the high priest.

Servant Girl: You also were with Jesus, the man from Nazareth.

Peter: I do not know or understand what you are talking about. *(A ROOSTER CROWS.)*

Servant Girl: This man is one of them.

Peter: No. You have me confused with somebody else.

Bystander: Certainly you are one of them; for you are a Galilean.

Peter: I do not know this man you are talking about. *(A ROOSTER CROWS.)*

Jesus: *(from off stage)* Before the cock crows twice, you will deny me three times.

Peter: *(Sits down and begins to cry.)*

Rooster's Tail

Laughing at someone's mistake.

Talking back to a parent.

Stealing something.

Bullying someone.

Picking a fight with a brother or sister.

Telling lies.

I Deny Jesus

1. A friend asks for help cheating on a math test because it's his worst subject, and I decide it's no big deal.

- -

2. I spread gossip about someone because I am angry at the person or just don't like the person.

- -

3. Someone offers me free drugs, and I decide to try them because my friends are taking them and just once won't hurt anything.

4. I never let anyone know I go to church or tell them I am a Christian, because they might laugh at me or because one of my teachers says there is no God.

- -

5. I lie to get myself out of trouble.

- -

6. I treat other people disrespectfully.

THE CRUCIFIXION

<table>
<tr>
<td>

Objectives
Older-elementary children and tweens will
- learn some details of what crucifixion was like
- create Holy Week symbols
- finish the three-dimensional Holy Week Road
- experience worship that includes the seven last words of Jesus

</td>
<td>

Bible Story
Mark 15:1-41: Jesus' trial, crucifixion, and death

Bible Verse
Mark 15:39b: Truly this man was God's Son!

</td>
</tr>
</table>

Focus for the Teacher

Jesus on Trial

Jesus' trail was one of humiliation and torture. Jesus was shunted back and forth while the religious authorities attempted to find a way to get the death penalty for him. They could not crucify him themselves, and yet they felt he was a direct threat not only to their authority but also to the survival of the Jewish people.

A broad overview of the arrest and trial will be part of today's lesson, but the core of the lesson will deal with Jesus' crucifixion.

The Crucifixion

Crucifixion was a painful, ugly, and humiliating process. It is time that older-elementary children and especially tweens understand what this meant. Knowing the suffering and death that Jesus endured is crucial to the understanding of just how great a reversal the Resurrection is. This is not a story of a super hero who almost dies because he came up against a superhuman villain and is brought back with a magic potion.

Jesus was a flesh-and-blood human being who suffered, was crucified, and died. He was raised

Truly this man was God's Son! Mark 15:39b

from the dead. All of this happened so that we might be saved and have eternal life.

This is abstract for older-elementary children and tweens. They don't have to understand everything all at once. But it's time they hear more than that Jesus died and then rose on the third day.

Easter's true meaning comes from the events of Good Friday. Older-elementary children and tweens—especially tweens—can take being serious if they think that something is truly important.

The Children

It is especially important for this lesson to be sensitive to the difference in maturity levels between older-elementary children and tweens. We have carefully crafted the small-group time to these age considerations. While all children this age may be able to talk in a sophisticated manner, there is a difference in their abilities to process abstract information.

For the interest groups, you will need to encourage them to split up, as only a few children can really work in each.

Explore Interest Groups

Be sure that adult teachers are waiting when the first child arrives. Greet and welcome each child. Get the child involved in an activity that interests him or her and introduces the theme for the day's activities. Encourage older-elementary children to make the Golgotha Hill and tweens to make the crosses and crown of thorns. **Explain that everyone will get to participate in eating the hot cross buns later.**

Make the Golgotha Hill (Older Elementary)

- **Say:** Today, we are going to hear of Jesus' trial and crucifixion. Jesus was crucified on a hill called Golgotha. We are going to make Golgotha Hill to go on our Holy Week Road.

- Have the children glue the flat side of one half of the styrofoam ball on a small piece of cardboard.

- Have them glue Easter basket grass all over the ball and cardboard. They may wish to add twigs and other things around the base of the "hill."

- Set the hill aside to dry to use during worship.

Make Crosses and a Crown of Thorns (Tweens)

- **Say:** Today, we are going to hear of Jesus' trial and crucifixion. Jesus was crucified between two thieves. He was taunted, and a crown of thorns was placed on his head. We are going to make the three crosses and the crown of thorns.

Directions for making crosses:

- Give three tweens some twigs and some twine or yarn.

- Have them find a thick twig for the upright portion of the cross and use a knife (under adult supervision) to cut small pieces from the bottom part to make a point so it can be pushed into styrofoam. Find another twig for the crossbar of the cross and, if necessary, break or cut it to size.

- They will have to help one another. One tween holds the sticks together. The other tween wraps twine or yarn around where the twigs come together, ties a knot to hold it in place, and continues crisscrossing the twine or yarn to hold the crossbar and the upright together.

Directions for making the crown of thorns:

- Trace the "Crown of Thorns Pattern" (page 56) onto a piece of felt.

- Cut around the outside of the circle, and then cut out the middle.

- Break toothpicks into shorter pieces, and glue them randomly around the circle (crown), making it look like the toothpicks are thorns.

- Set the crosses and the crown of thorns aside to dry to use during worship.

NOTE: Any extra crosses and/or crowns of thorns may be placed around the room or sent home.

Prepare

✓ Cut a fairly good-sized styrofoam ball in half. (A bread knife works well.)

✓ Cut a square of cardboard large enough so that the styrofoam ball fits on it and has room around it for the base of the "hill."

✓ Provide half a styrofoam ball; square piece of cardboard; craft glue; Easter basket grass; twigs, small gravel, or leaves.

Prepare

✓ Photocopy the "Crown of Thorns Pattern" (page 56), and cut off the top of the page.

✓ Provide twigs, twine or dark-colored yarn, knife (to be used only under adult supervision), marker, scissors, brown or black felt, toothpicks, glue.

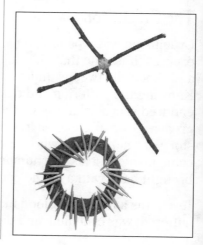

Ice Hot Cross Buns (All)

- Put out enough buns or rolls for everyone to have one. Keep a basic sugar icing warm in a crockpot.

- **Say:** Eating hot cross buns on Good Friday is a tradition of the Christian church that goes back a long time. It symbolizes Jesus' death on the cross. We are going to ice buns for everyone. Spread the warm icing in the form of a cross.

- Make sure the children use hand sanitizer to clean their hands.

- Give everyone a plastic or butter knife, and ask them to do the following:

  * Spread icing on each bun in the form of a cross.

  * Put the finished buns on napkins or small plates and then put them on trays for serving.

  * Clean up the area when finished.

Prepare

✓ Make or purchase enough buns for everyone to have one. (Find a recipe on the Internet, or purchase prepackaged cinnamon roll dough and bake it.)

✓ Set up a crockpot containing a simple sugar icing to warm.

✓ Provide hand sanitizer, buns, small plates or napkins, serving trays, plastic or butter knives, and warm icing.

Bible Story Presentation Practice (All)

- Explain that today's story is important and that it needs to be read well. The readings have been divided up and must be read in order.

- Give everyone a Bible.

- Pass out the "Trial and Crucifixion" assignments (page 53).

- There are twelve assignments. Give one or more assignments to each reader, depending on the number of readers you have.

- Have the readers look up each assignment and mark it in their Bibles, using the assignment papers.

- Give them time to read their part (or parts) to themselves several times.

- Bring all of the children together, and make sure that everyone understands which order their parts come in. Ask them to read as dramatically as possible. Remind them to speak loudly so that everyone can hear them.

- Explain that their chairs will be in a row in front of everyone. When it is their turn to read, they will quietly stand up, read, and then quietly sit down. If they have more than one part, they will stand for each reading and sit in between readings.

Prepare

✓ Photocopy and cut apart the "Trial and Crucifixion" assignments (page 53).

✓ Provide Bibles and "Trial and Crucifixion" reproducible.

Symbol Game (All)

- Mix up the "Symbol Cards," and lay them face-down in rows on a table.

- **Say:** Symbols are reminders of important things. Let's see how many Lenten symbols you remember.

- Play a simple matching game with the cards with one twist. If someone matches two cards, he or she must state what the symbol means before keeping the pair.

Prepare

✓ Photocopy and cut apart two sets of the "Symbol Cards" (page 54).

✓ Provide two sets of cut-apart "Symbol Cards."

Large Group

Bring all older-elementary children and tweens together to experience the Bible story. Ring a bell or play music to alert everyone to the large-group time. Use the transition activity to move the children from the interest groups to the large-group area.

Eat Hot Cross Buns

- Have the children wash their hands (or use hand sanitizer) and move to an open area of the room where they can eat.

- Ask those who iced the buns to serve them, making sure that everyone gets one and a cup of water or juice.

- **Say:** Eating hot cross buns on Good Friday is a tradition of the Christian church that goes back a long time. It symbolizes Jesus' death on the cross.

- Let everyone eat. Have wet wipes available to clean sticky hands.

Prepare
✓ Provide hand sanitizer, plates or napkins, buns (iced earlier), cups, water or juice, wet wipes.

CAUTION: Be aware of food allergies the children have.

Bible Readings

- While the children are finishing their buns, move chairs for the readers in a row facing the children.

- When ready, have those who will be reading the Bible come forward and sit in the chairs.

- **Say:** Jesus came into Jerusalem on Sunday, riding on a donkey. The crowd laid palm branches and cloaks before him and shouted, "Hosanna!" But things quickly changed. On Thursday, Jesus and the disciples shared the Passover meal in the Upper Room, where Jesus instituted Communion and said he would be betrayed and denied. Jesus then took Peter, James, and John with him to the garden of Gethsemane, where he prayed. When he had finished praying, he was confronted by a crowd. Judas betrayed Jesus with a kiss, and Jesus was arrested and taken before the council. All the disciples deserted Jesus. Peter, who had followed Jesus at a distance, denied knowing Jesus. It is here we pick up the story.

- Ask the first reader to begin. Be prepared to signal each reader's turn.

- Take the final collection of socks for people who are homeless and prepare them for donation.

- Dismiss the children to their small groups.

Prepare
✓ Provide Bibles, "Trial and Crucifixion" assignments (which were handed out during "Bible Story Presentation Practice"), and the box for collecting socks.

Small Groups

Divide the children into small groups. The best division is between older elementary and tweens (or sophistication level). Keep the groups small, with a maximum of ten children in each group. You may need to have more than one of each group.

Older Elementary

- Have older-elementary children sit around a table with craft supplies.

- **Say:** Luke 23:44-45 says that when Jesus died, "It was now about noon, and darkness came over the whole land until three in the afternoon, while the sun's light failed; and the curtain of the temple was torn in two." It was a very dark day. We heard read just moments ago that when Jesus died a Roman centurion who was there to act as a guard was greatly moved. He recognized that Jesus is the Son of God.

- Give each child a copy of "Mark 15:39b" (page 55).

- Encourage the children to use white or yellow crayons to outline the verse and the crosses.

- Have them cover the entire picture with diluted black tempera paint. This will allow the white or yellow to show through.

- Set the pictures aside to dry so that the children can take them home.

- Have the children clean their hands with wet wipes or water.

- **Say:** It was a dark and terrible day when Jesus died. But we know that Jesus is our light. He died for us. He is truly God's Son.

- Ask two of those who prepared the Golgotha Hill to prepare to set it on the Holy Week Road at a signal from you.

- Ask everyone to gather in the worship area.

Tweens

- Have tweens gather and sit in a circle or around a table.

- **Say:** Jesus was crucified. Crucifixion was a horrible form of death. Here are some facts about crucifixion:
    1. The Romans crucified only slaves, non-Romans, those who made trouble for the government, and the lowest form of criminals.
    2. A person was whipped with a whip with leather thongs, which would have weakened the person.
    3. A condemned man was made to carry the cross arm of the cross to his place of crucifixion. This would have been very heavy.
    4. A person was stripped of his clothes before crucifixion.
    5. The nails were probably driven through the wrists. According to archaeological finds, the knees were usually bent and one foot placed on top of the other before the nail was driven through the feet.

Prepare

- ✓ Cover a table with a cloth or old newspaper to protect it.

- ✓ Photocopy "Mark 15:39b" (page 55) for each child.

- ✓ Provide "Mark 15:39b" reproducible, white or yellow crayons, black tempera paint diluted with water, paintbrushes, water and towels or wet wipes to clean hands.

Prepare

- ✓ Photocopy and cut apart the "Seven Last Words of Jesus" (page 56).

- ✓ Give the "Words of Dismissal" reproducible (page 4) to a tween volunteer.

- ✓ Make sure that the crosses and crown of thorns are ready for worship.

- ✓ Provide "Seven Last Words of Jesus" and "Words of Dismissal" reproducibles.

- **Say:** Jesus spoke seven times from the cross. Today, we are preparing for a special worship. We will read those seven words, so we are going to spend the next few minutes preparing for the group worship.

- Hand out the "Seven Last Words of Jesus" (page 56), each to a different tween. (If you have a small group, multiple assignments may be given.)

- Give one tween the "Words of Dismissal."

- **Say:** Jesus was crucified on Golgotha between two thieves. The older-elementary children will be placing Golgotha Hill on the Holy Week Road. We will be adding the three crosses on Golgotha.

- Assign three tweens to place, during worship, the crosses into the top of Golgotha and one to place the crown of thorns at the foot of Golgotha.

- Explain that the three crosses will have to be gently pushed into the styrofoam in order to stand upright.

- Explain that the readers will stand at the back of the group to read. The Scriptures must be read in the right order.

- Tweens without an assignment may set up chairs in the worship area.

- Go through the order of worship:
  * The Golgotha Hill will be placed on the road.
  * During the first two readings, the three crosses will be placed on Golgotha Hill and the crown of thorns will be placed at the bottom of the hill.
  * The readings will continue as everyone sits in silence.
  * The "Words of Dismissal" will be read.

- When everyone is sure of their directions, ask them to gather in the worship area, with the readers standing in the back.

Large-Group Worship

Bring everyone together for a time of closing worship. Much of what you have done during this lesson leads up to worship, so it is a critical part of the lesson.

- Explain that worship will be done in silence, except for the assigned spoken parts.

- Signal for the Golgotha Hill to be brought forward and placed on the Holy Week Road.

- Signal for the first reading to begin and for those with the crosses and crown of thorns to come forward and place them.

- Keep track of the readings, signaling if necessary to the next reader.

- When the readings are finished, signal for everyone to bow their heads for prayer and for the "Words of Dismissal" to be read.

- Signal that it is time for everyone to collect their things and leave in silence.

Prepare
✓ Provide "Seven Last Words of Jesus" assignments, "Words of Dismissal" reproducible, and items made for the Holy Week Road.

Trial and Crucifixion

Mark 15:1-5
Mark 15:8-9
Mark 15:11
Mark 15:15
Mark 15:16
Mark 15:20
Mark 15:21-24
Mark 15:25-28
Mark 15:33
Mark 15:34
Mark 15:36-37
Mark 15:38-39

Symbol Cards

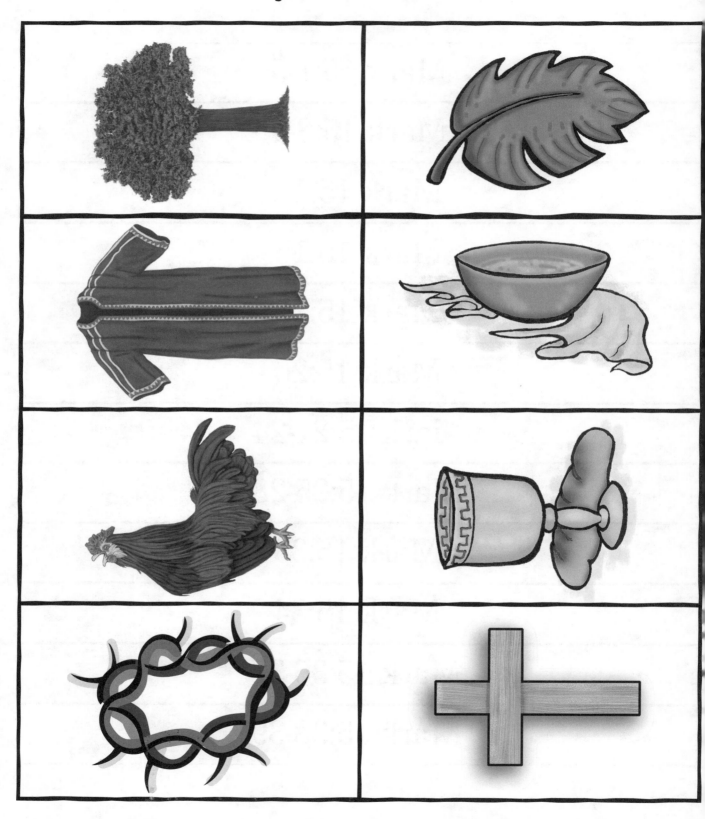

24 Hours That Changed the World (For Older Children)

Mark 15:39b

truly this man was God's Son! mark 15:39b

Seven Last Words of Jesus

1. They crucified Jesus there with the criminals, one on his right and one on his left. Then Jesus said, "Father, forgive them; for they do not know what they are doing." (Luke 23:33-34)

2. One of the criminals derided Jesus… But the other rebuked him. He said, "Jesus, remember me when you come into your kingdom." Jesus replied, "Truly I tell you, today you will be with me in Paradise." (Luke 23:39-43, adapted)

3. When Jesus saw his mother and the disciple whom he loved standing beside her, he said to his mother, "Woman, here is your son." Then he said to the disciple, "Here is your mother." (John 19:26-27a)

4. At three o'clock Jesus cried out with a loud voice, "…My God, my God, why have you forsaken me?" (Mark 15:34)

5. When Jesus knew that all was now finished, he said (in order to fulfill the scripture), "I am thirsty." (John 19:28)

6. When Jesus had received the wine, he said, "It is finished." (John 19:30a)

7. It was now about noon, and darkness came over the whole land until three in the afternoon, while the sun's light failed; and the curtain of the temple was torn in two. Then Jesus, crying with a loud voice, said, "Father, into your hands I commend my spirit." Having said this, he breathed his last. (Luke 23:44-46)

Crown of Thorns Pattern (see page 48)

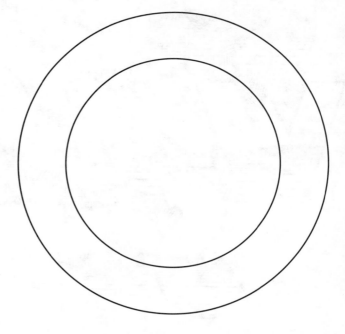

24 Hours That Changed the World (For Older Children)

7 THE RESURRECTION

Objectives
Older-elementary children and tweens will
• read the Resurrection story
• be introduced to the meaning of Resurrection
• replace Holy Week Road with Easter Cross
• experience celebratory worship

Bible Story
Mark 16:1-6: The empty tomb

Bible Verse
Mark 16:6c, d: He has been raised; he is not here.

Focus for the Teacher

Jesus' Triumph Over Death

The tone of today's lesson will be very different from the sadness of the preceding lessons. We have gone through Jesus' triumphal entry into Jerusalem, arrest, trial, and finally his crucifixion and death.

Jesus had been buried hastily due to the Jewish custom of burying the body on the day of death. Jesus died late in the afternoon, which made it more difficult to prepare him properly.

The women arrived at the tomb with the spices necessary to properly bury the dead. They were alarmed when they saw a young man in a white robe, who told them that Jesus had been raised. Jesus had told them he would rise, but they had seen him die and did not have Jesus' understanding of the ways of God.

What It Means to Us

Now it is time to put Jesus' suffering and death in Christian perspective. God was willing to come in human form to suffer and die, that we might have redemption and eternal life. These concepts are still abstract even for tweens, but they need to hear the words and learn the language. As they grow in faith and understanding, they will come to know what it means for their own lives.

What does it mean? It means that if we are willing to accept it, we are being offered forgiveness and salvation. Salvation from what? We are being offered salvation from ourselves. In looking out for "number one," we often forget God and do things that are harmful to ourselves and others. The resurrection of Jesus offers us a new relationship with God, a relationship that does not require us to suffer as Jesus did, but instead gives us the opportunity to accept a better way of life. This gives us the possibility of eternal life.

With older-elementary children, the lesson will center on the joy of the good news of Jesus' resurrection. With tweens, who are beginning to think somewhat abstractly, there will be a look at the promise of eternal life.

> He has been raised; he is not here.
> Mark 16:6c, d

Explore Interest Groups

Be sure that adult teachers are waiting when the first child arrives. Greet and welcome each child. Get the child involved in an activity that interests him or her and introduces the theme for the day's activities. All interest group activities today are appropriate for both older-elementary children and tweens.

Remove the Holy Week Road (All)

- **Say:** On the third day, Jesus was raised from the dead. Today, we are going to celebrate the Resurrection. The symbols of Lent are not appropriate for the Easter season, so we are going to remove them in preparation for Easter worship.

- Explain where and how things on the Holy Week Road are going to be disposed of (or moved to a central location in the church where the display can be seen by others).

- Have the children choose which part (or parts) each will remove before beginning. This will help keep confusion to a minimum.

- Have everything removed and disposed of as you have explained.

- Adults and children can work together to remove the table or, if the cross is going to sit on the table, to cover the table with a white cloth or plain white paper.

Prepare

- ✓ Make a decision about whether the Holy Week Road will be put on display somewhere (and how to move it) or be torn down.

- ✓ Provide a white cloth or plain white paper if you plan to cover the table.

Assembly-Line Butterflies (All)

- **Say:** On the third day, Jesus was raised from the dead. Today, we are going to celebrate the Resurrection. The symbols of Lent are not appropriate for the Easter season, so we are going to remove them. Since butterflies are the symbol for new life, we are going to make butterflies for everyone to attach to the cross during our Easter worship.

- Have the children spread out along a table. You may have as many assembly lines as the number of children permits.

- Give the first child in line a stack of tissue paper in various colors, a small paper plate, a pencil, and a pair of scissors. This child puts the paper plate on a piece of tissue paper, traces around the paper plate, and cuts out the circle. This child puts the tissue paper circle pattern on several pieces of tissue paper at a time and then cuts them out.

- Give the second child a stack of tissue paper in various colors, a round object that is about two inches smaller in diameter than the paper plate, a pencil, and a pair of scissors. This child puts the round object on a piece of tissue paper, traces around the object, and cuts out the circle. This child puts the tissue paper circle pattern on several pieces of tissue paper at a time and then cuts them out.

- Give the third child chenille stems. This child bends one chenille stem in half, twists it securely three or four times about two inches from the top (folded end), and gives it to the fourth child.

Prepare

- ✓ Provide tissue paper (various colors), small paper plate, round object that is two inches smaller in diameter than the paper plate (such as a coffee can), chenille stems, pencils, scissors.

- The fourth child takes a small circle, folds it in half, twists the center, puts it between the two parts of the chenille stem, and then does the same thing with the large circle. This child twists the chenille stem once to hold the "wings" in place.

- The last child takes the butterfly and makes a twist toward the end of the chenille stem to form the head and the antennae. This child lays the butterfly aside for later.

- Repeat until enough butterflies are made for everyone in attendance.

Bible Verse Tangram (All)

- **Say:** We're going to work a puzzle that when solved will tell us something about Jesus.

- Give each child a copy of "Easter Tangram" and some scissors.

- Have them cut out their tans. (Tans are the shapes.)

- **Say:** The shapes will fit only one way onto the puzzle. If you put them in the puzzle correctly, you will discover today's Bible verse.

- Have them attempt to work the puzzle.

- Check each puzzle to make sure the answer is correct. *(The answer is on page 64.)*

- When a child has finished the puzzle, he or she may help another child if help is needed.

"Where Is Jesus?" Egg Hunt (All)

- Open plastic Easter eggs and insert the Mark Bible verse strip in all but one of them. In that one egg, put the Luke verse (about Jesus' ascension into heaven).

- Hide the eggs around the area, making sure the one with the Luke verse is difficult to find.

- **Say:** On Easter morning, the women discovered that Jesus' tomb was empty. We're going to discover where Jesus is.

- Explain that when they find where Jesus is, they are to return with the egg. (Only one should be returning, since only one egg says where Jesus is. The other eggs say where he is not.)

- When the answer has been found, call everyone back together and have the verse read.

- **Say:** Jesus has gone before us to prepare the way for us. But we are never alone. God in three persons—God the Father, God the Son, and God the Holy Spirit—is always with us.

Prepare
✓ Photocopy "Easter Tangram" (page 63) for each child, and cut off the bottom of the page.

✓ Provide "Easter Tangram" reproducible and scissors for each child.

Prepare
✓ Obtain plastic Easter eggs.

✓ Photocopy and cut apart the "Bible Verse Strips" (page 63). You will need one copy of the Luke verse and multiple copies of the Mark verse (one per egg).

✓ Put the strips inside of the eggs (one Luke verse, all others the Mark verse).

✓ Hide the eggs around the area, making sure the one with the Luke verse is difficult to find.

Large Group

Bring all older-elementary children and tweens together to experience the Bible story. Ring a bell or play music to alert everyone to the large-group time. Use the transition activity to move the children from the interest groups to the large-group area.

"Christ Is Risen" Ball Toss

Prepare
✓ Provide balls (one for each group).

- Have everyone move to an open area of the room.

- Depending on the size of the group, have them form one or more circles.

- **Say:** In many Christian churches, even today, Christians begin worship with the words "Christ is risen!" and the response "Christ is risen indeed!"

- Explain that you will give each group a ball. The first child is to toss the ball to another child and say the child's name and "Christ is risen!" The child who catches the ball is to reply with the name of the child who tossed the ball and "Christ is risen indeed!" Continue tossing the ball and repeating the greeting and response.

NOTE: If you have a large group of children who do not know one another's names, you may omit the use of names and just repeat the greetings.

- Play until everyone has received the ball and tossed it at least once.

Hear and Remember the Bible Story

Prepare
✓ Provide a Bible, pencils, and paper.

- Ask all the children to sit facing you. Give each child a pencil and paper.

- **Say:** I'm going to read today's Bible story. You will have to listen carefully, because a lot of things happen and I'm going to be asking you about them.

- Read Mark 16:1-6.

- Ask everyone to work in groups of three or four to write the answers to the questions. When done, you'll check to see which group has the greatest number of correct answers.

Questions:

1. Who brought spices to the tomb? *(Mary Magdalene, Mary the mother of James, and Salome)*

2. What did they find at the entrance to the tomb? *(The stone had been rolled away.)*

3. Whom did they see? *(a young man, who was dressed in a white robe)*

4. What side was he sitting on? *(the right side)*

5. What did he say? *(Any part of verse six is acceptable.)*

- Check the answers, and then send the children to small groups.

24 Hours That Changed the World (For Older Children)

Small Groups

Divide the children into small groups. The best division is between older elementary and tweens (or sophistication level). Keep the groups small, with a maximum of ten children in each group. You may need to have more than one of each group.

Older-Elementary Children

- Have the children sit in a circle or at a table where they can see the dry-erase board or large sheet of paper you have posted.

- **Say:** When we have good news, we like to share it. We share the things that are important to us with others.

- **Ask:** If something really exciting happened to you, whom would you tell first?

- Record their answers.

- **Say:** If we had read the ending of Mark, we would have discovered that those who had seen Jesus told the other disciples. That is, they told their friends. Later, after Pentecost, they told a lot of other people.

- **Ask:** Who else do we tell when we have exciting news?

- Record their answers.

- **Say:** Our actions tell everyone what we really believe. If we believe what Jesus taught us, we will treat others well and show God's love.

- **Ask:** Whom could we add to our list of people that we can share God's love with through our actions?

- Record their answers.

- Explain that everyone will be given a butterfly to attach to the cross during worship.

- Dismiss the children to go to the worship area.

Tweens

- Ask the tweens to sit in groups of three or four.

- Give each group a pencil and paper.

- **Say:** The exciting news of Jesus' resurrection is that it brings the promise of eternal life to all of us. Let's think about what the word *eternal* means. When I tell you to begin, you will have three minutes to make a list of things that seem eternal, things that were here before you and will probably be here long after you are gone (mountains, rocks, oceans, solar system, and so forth).

- Give the signal.

- After three minutes, bring everyone back together, and let them report on what they came up with.

Prepare
- ✓ Set up an area with a dry-erase board and marker or large sheet of paper and marker.

Prepare
- ✓ Give the "Easter Prayer" reproducible (page 4) to a tween volunteer.

- ✓ Provide Bibles, paper, and pencils.

- **Say:** Last week, we talked about death, specifically the death of Jesus. People die and will continue to die. However, because of the death and resurrection of Jesus Christ, we know that death is not the end. Life goes on in another, more exciting form—a life with God.

- Give every tween a Bible.

- **Say:** I will give you a Bible reference, and you will race to see who can find the Bible verse first. The first one to find it will stand. Remain standing while I give another reference. When I give the second reference, those seated will race to find the second Bible verse. When that verse is found, the second person stands. These two remain standing while the others look for another Bible verse. When all verses have been found, those standing will read their verses.

- Read these references for the Bible verse race: Romans 5:8; Romans 6:23; 1 John 2:25; John 3:16; John 3:17.

- Have those standing read their verses in the order given.

- Explain that everyone will be given a butterfly to attach to the cross during worship.

- Ask one volunteer to read Mark 16:6 during worship, and give another volunteer the "Easter Prayer" (page 4) to read.

- Dismiss everyone to go to the worship area

Large-Group Worship

Bring everyone together for a time of closing worship. Much of what you have done during this lesson leads up to worship, so it is a critical part of the lesson.

- Have everyone sit in the worship area in front of the cross.
- Ask those who made the butterflies to pass them out, one for each child.
- Also give everyone a pin or tack to attach their butterflies to the cross.
- **Say:** The butterfly is a symbol of new life in Jesus Christ. We all have that promise of eternal life and are holding a symbol of that promise. After the reading of the Bible verse, we will each pin our butterflies to the empty cross.
- Ask the volunteer to read the Bible verse.
- Ask the children to come forward and pin their butterflies to the cross.
- After everyone has returned to their seats, close by having the volunteer read the "Easter Prayer."

Prepare

✓ While the children are in the interest groups at the beginning of the lesson, place a large cross made of styrofoam or of wood at the front of the worship area.

✓ Make sure every child has a butterfly and a pin or tack.

✓ Provide a Bible and the "Easter Prayer" reproducible.

Easter Tangram

Bible Verse Strips

He has been raised; he is not here. (Mark 16:6c, d)

While he was blessing them, he withdrew from them and was carried up into heaven. (Luke 24:51)

Answers

Lesson 1: "Names for Jesus" Crossword

ACROSS
1. Emmanuel
4. Son of God
5. Savior
6. Teacher
7. Lord

DOWN
2. Messiah
3. Son of David

Lesson 1: Beginning and End

MATCHING
Alpha and Omega (beginning and end)
The Bread of Life
The Good Shepherd
Lamb of God
Light of the World
Prince of Peace
Son of David
Son of God
Wonderful Counselor

OTHER NAMES
Savior
Messiah
Lord

Lesson 4: Who Prayed Where?

Anna—in the Temple
Daniel—in an upper room with open windows
Early Christians—in home of Mary, the Mother of Mark
Jonah—in the belly of a large fish

Lesson 7: Easter Tangram

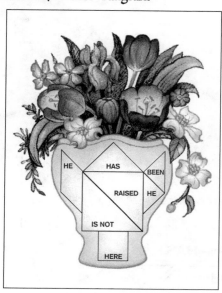

Lesson 4: Why Did They Pray?

SCRIPTURE	WHO PRAYED	PRAYED FOR	REQUEST
Genesis 18:23-24	Abraham	righteous people of Sodom	save city if a righteous man could be found
Numbers 12:10-13	Moses	Miriam	for recovery from leprosy
1 Kings 3:9-10	Solomon	himself	an understanding mind to be a better king
Luke 23:33-34	Jesus	those who crucified him	God's forgiveness for their actions
Acts 12:5	early church	Peter	release from prison
Ephesians 3:14-19	Paul	the Ephesian church (readers of the letter)	to strengthen their faith

24 Hours That Changed the World (For Older Children)